When 'End of Life Care' Goes Wrong

A Report from
the Lords and Commons Family
and Child Protection Group

Editor
Robert S. Harris

Executive Editor
Revd. Lynda Rose

Published by
Voice for Justice UK

Published in Great Britain in 2023 by Voice for Justice UK
PO Box 8893 OX1 9PY

*Voice for Justice UK works to uphold and defend human rights, and to be a
voice for those who cannot speak for themselves. Interested readers are
invited to consult the website for details of its activities at*

www.vfjuk.org.uk

Voice for Justice UK ISBN 978-0-9929964-4-4

Printed in Great Britain by Imprint Digital, Exeter

Contents

Preface

What does it mean to die well? Some argue that it's having freedom of choice in end of life options, others that it's simply allowing nature to 'take its course', surrounded, hopefully, by loved ones. All would hopefully agree that the process should be free of coercion, whether that's from receiving treatment the individual doesn't want; from having such treatment withdrawn without the knowledge, consent, or agreement of the patient or of his or her family; or from measures being put in place, possibly again without knowledge or consent, that will actively hasten death, on the spurious grounds that it's in the best interests of the patient, and will alleviate unnecessary suffering.

In 2014, in face of mounting complaint and pressure, the now notorious Liverpool Care Pathway was withdrawn. The LCP, as it was popularly known, professed to provide guidelines for best practice in end of life care, focusing on symptom control, combined, where appropriate, with the discontinuation of active treatments no longer judged to be of use. In support of which, it aimed to provide individualized psychological, social and spiritual care for patients and their families, framed round frequent patient reassessment, that could be easily and speedily changed in response to need.

It sounded wonderful! Yet, in practice, the Pathway was a disaster. The British media went so far as to label it a licence to kill, calling it a 'pathway to euthanasia' and claiming that, far from operating in the best interests of patients, the withdrawal of food and oral hydration, combined with heavy sedation, were measures that were designed to kill.[1] Many complained that the Pathway was a harsh and uncaring tick box system that led to premature death, whose primary function was not to ensure uniformly good care for those facing their last days, but rather intended to free up hospital beds in an over-strained system of health care. Alarm bells really began to ring, however, when it was revealed that hospitals were being offered massive financial incentives to ensure that between a third to two thirds of all deaths of patients under their care should be as result of the controversial pathway.[2]

The independent review, *More Care, Less Pathway*, commissioned in 2013 by Norman Lamb MP, at the time Minister of State for Community and

Social Care, and chaired by Baroness Neuberger, was an attempt to find out if there was any substance to the allegations. Its findings were alarming.[3] Though it was acknowledged that, used properly, many patients on the Pathway had a 'good' and peaceful death, it reported that elsewhere there was clear evidence of poor treatment, and even malpractice, with patients being treated without respect and subjected to treatments that designedly gave no benefit, but caused manifest distress and harm – such as the almost routine withdrawal of oral hydration. It further found that such treatments not only served to hurry along the inevitable, but were sometimes put in place for patients who would otherwise have recovered.

Overall, the review identified repeated failures to communicate either properly or fully with patients and/or with their relatives or carers, sometimes indeed wrongly recording prior consultation and agreement, when it was known that no discussion had taken place. In part, it was believed this was the result of confusion amongst medical staff over whether or not the pathway should be classified as medical treatment – requiring the patient's consent – or more properly viewed as a justifiable decision on the part of clinicians, to be 'taken in the patient's best interests'. Either way, on repeated occasions evidence was given that, in a best interest assessment, clinicians had failed properly to seek consent from a patient, or to consult with relatives, when considering a changed approach to treatment, and had simply gone ahead. With entirely predictable results.

Relatives, who gave evidence, also expressed the view that drugs were being used as a "chemical cosh", rendering the patient comatose, while unnecessarily diminishing the desire or ability to accept food or drink. Such blatant lack of genuine care was criticised as unwarranted and cruel.

Perhaps unsurprisingly, following the report's damning assessment, the Pathway was withdrawn, replaced by a range of friendlier sounding 'end of life care' packages. Sadly, however, though the name changed, the practices continued, leading to a continued stream of complaints from aggrieved relatives. Specifically, that their loved ones had been deliberately killed by inappropriate withdrawal of food and hydration and prescription of strong sedatives, whose only purpose was to render the patient unconscious and hasten death. In recent years, such complaints, often leading to Coroners' inquiries and legal action – and sometimes even criminal investigation – have, unfortunately, become commonplace.

It is against this background of mounting anger and complaint on the part of bereaved relatives that the Lords and Commons Family and Child Protection Group commissioned the current report, *When 'end of life care' goes wrong*. It should be said that when care for the dying works well, it is superb, and we unreservedly applaud the dedicated medical staff, and unpaid carers, who deliver professional, skilled and compassionate end of life care. But the impetus for this report was the overwhelming evidence of situations where this fails to happen, and where the care received continues to 'go wrong'.

Knowing the deep upset felt by those who have lost loved ones as result of what they feel to be inappropriate treatment deliberately designed to hasten death, we agreed from the start strict parameters for the inclusion of cases. First, we requested documentary evidence from all those who submitted case studies and we thank those who went to great lengths to supply this. Where available, our medical expert has scrutinised these and has offered his explanation, opinions and conclusions. Another requirement was that the case studies had to demonstrate violation of ethical and legal guidelines put in place for the regulation and governance of end of life care.

The 16 case studies included fulfil those requirements – but they are only the tip of a very large iceberg. The stories they tell are heart-wrenching. For their sakes, but also for the thousands of grief-stricken relatives with similar stories, not included here, as well as for those who will face similar situations in the future, it is imperative that we address the confusion, lack of proper training and, in some cases, outright abuse that have deprived patients of proper care, as they approach the end of life. Most especially, it is vital that Parliamentarians be alerted to the abuses going on in hospitals and other care settings, so that action may be taken to end violations, provide proper training, and ensure delivery of compassionate care that will allow people to die with dignity and at peace.

We are indebted to those who have so courageously shared their stories, including those who have shared stories that, for whatever reason, were not included. As said above, our guidelines were tight, but this is in no way to belittle what they shared. The deep trauma and pain left by such experiences should not be underestimated, and revisiting the wounds, while being subjected to the scrutiny we have required, has taken both resolution and valour. Our thanks go too to Emeritus Professor Sam H Ahmedzai FRCP, who not only has over thirty years' experience in cancer and palliative medicine, but chaired the 2015 NICE committee for the care of dying adults and acted as Clinical Adviser to the 2019 NICE NG142 guideline on service delivery for people in the last year of life. Prof Ahmedzai has scrutinised, critically evaluated, and commented on every report – an enormous and time-consuming labour of love for which we are deeply grateful.

Our thanks go also to barrister and medical law specialist James Bogle, for his clear analysis of clinical violations in end of life care and the failure of compliance.

It remains to thank Robert S Harris, who has worked so tirelessly to bring together and edit this report, and without whom it would most definitely not exist. With special thanks too to Alice Jones, for her editorial assistance; to Professor Patrick Pullicino and Denise Charlesworth-Smith, who introduced us to so many of the people featured in this report; and to Louise Kirk, Teresa Lynch and Nikki Kenward, for their further introductions and unremitting support.

In the NHS, we have a system that has rightly been called the envy of the world. Yet, as with all things in life, it is not perfect. Whatever our condition of life, every life matters – and every last moment of life is important for those bound together by love. There are a great many people in the medical and caring professions who recognize and practice this. But, unfortunately, not all. As a nation, we can do so much 'better' than the sham compassion that is all too often demonstrated in our care for those at the end of life. And we all need to know that when our own time comes, as for each and every one of us it most assuredly will, we shall receive the best care that our society can offer.

May we now work together to make that happen.

Lynda Rose
Convenor, the Lords and Commons Family and Child Protection Group

---

[1] https://www.dailymail.co.uk/news/article-2217061/Liverpool-Care-Pathway-Family-revive-man-doctors-wasnt-worth-saving.html

[2] https://www.dailymail.co.uk/news/article-2223286/Hospitals-bribed-patients-pathway-death-Cash-incentive-NHS-trusts-meet-targets-Liverpool-Care-Pathway.html

[3] https://assets.publishing.service.gov.uk/government/uploads/system/uploads/attachment_data/file/212450/Liverpool_Care_Pathway.pdf

Foreword

In 1977, former United States' Vice President, Hubert Humphrey, said in a speech delivered in Washington, that the treatment of the weakest members of society is the real test and reflection of a government's moral standing. He said, "the moral test of government is how that government treats those who are in the dawn of life, the children; those who are in the twilight of life, the elderly; those who are in the shadows of life; the sick, the needy and the handicapped."

The LCFCPG report, *When 'end of life care' goes wrong*, deals specifically with the latter two groups, exposing what one is tempted to label the 'callous and inhumane treatment' meted out to some patients as they approach the end of life. Treatments such as the withdrawal of oral hydration – even when the patient is sometimes begging for a drink – or the administration of strong sedatives, prescribed with the sole intention of rendering the patient unconscious, while hastening death.

The Liverpool Care Pathway may have been officially scrapped in 2014, but the practices so unequivocally condemned appear to be continuing, albeit under different names? The current system is not just *not working*, but is a continuation of the practices withdrawn as not fit for purpose. It is urgent that Parliamentarians be alerted to the failure of care for the dying, evident in hospitals and other care settings, and that we act to stop all such abuse.

Hubert Humphrey rightly pointed out that such practices have no place in a 'civilised' society. All of us will one day face death. We must ensure that those who face crossing this frontier today are listened to, and accorded respect. That they are treated with genuine compassion and care.

I warmly commend this unsettling, but timely, report to all Parliamentarians, and urge that action be taken to stop such inhumane practices.

Carla Lockhart MP

When 'end of life care' goes wrong

Executive Summary

Following public outcry over the staggering number of premature and inappropriate deaths caused by the now infamous Liverpool Care Pathway (LCP), in 2014 the protocol was scrapped, presumably consigned to a scrapheap of medical mistakes from which it was hoped it would never again emerge. That hope proved to be misplaced. When end of life care in the NHS performs correctly, it is superb, but sadly, as this Report shows, the many-headed hydra that was the Pathway has refused to lie down. The name may have changed, but the misapplication, misuse – and even abuse – persist.

As this Report shows, misdiagnoses and mis-assessments as to quality of life are all too common. This, together with a failure to appreciate the respect and care required for those approaching their last days is, in every sense, a fatal combination. Excessive and inappropriate use of Midazolam and Morphine, rendering a patient comatose, coupled with the withdrawal of food and hydration, have combined to impose a death sentence from which, in the current climate, there is no right of appeal.

From over 600 complaints that we know about – the tip of a very large iceberg – this Report details 16 medically analysed and validated accounts of such failure, provided in their own words by families left stunned at the inhumane treatment suffered by their relations. The individualised 'care package', recommended by NICE in the wake of the LCP, has all too often become a pathway to death – imposed for what sometimes started out as seemingly trivial conditions. One patient, for example, was admitted for treatment for constipation. Others, otherwise healthy, underwent knee replacement surgery or elective eye surgery.

Commentary on each case is provided by Professor Emeritus Sam H Ahmedzai FRCP, a palliative medicine specialist, who chaired the NICE guideline committee responsible for its clinical guidance on care for the dying adult in 2015. Legal analysis is provided by James Bogle, a practising barrister specialising in clinical negligence, and especially end of life cases.

Examining the many clinical failures, and what sometimes appears blatant abuse, the Report concludes with a series of proposed actions to address the problems.

We propose the following:

1. A national inventory of local end of life care plans, policies and procedures currently being used in all healthcare settings

2. A national rapid response service to advise and support people who have a loved one currently experiencing poor quality end of life care

3. A fast track advice helpline for recently bereaved families

4. A national register of cases where end of life care has fallen below standards or breaches guidelines

5. The urgent adoption of a uniform national system to capture patients' preferences for end of life care

6. Further high quality research into social, medical and nursing aspects of end of life care

Doctors are called to save life, not kill, and it is urgent these problems be addressed by Parliament, and appropriate action taken to end such callous and inhumane treatment of those at the end of life.

Biographies

Emeritus Professor Sam H Ahmedzai BSc (Hons) MBChB FRCP FFPM

Sam is Emeritus Professor at the University of Sheffield, with 30 years' experience of being an academic physician in palliative medicine, covering both acute hospital and hospice. His research interests include: pain and symptom management; supportive care throughout cancer; quality of life measurement; patient and public involvement in research. He was a founding member of the Association for Palliative Medicine and set up the APM Science Committee. He chaired the guideline committee for the 2015 NICE *NG31 guideline for care of the dying adult* and was clinical adviser to the 2019 NICE *NG142 guideline on service delivery* for people in the last year of life. He was specialist committee member on NICE Quality Standards QS13 and QS144 on end of life care. He was chair of the 2016 RCP National Audit of Care at the end of life in hospital. In 2016, Sam was given the Lifetime Achievement Award by the British Thoracic Oncology Group.

James Bogle

James Bogle is a barrister of the Middle Temple of some 30 years standing in private practice. His practice embraces health and public law, commercial law, and property law. He has appeared in a number of high profile medically-related public law cases including *Barts Health NHS Trust v Dance* [2022] in the High Court (involving a 12 year-old boy, Archie Battersbee), *University Hospitals Plymouth NHS Trust v RS, Z, M, S and R [2021]* in the Court of Protection, *Z v RS* [2021] in the Court of Appeal, *R (Smeaton) v Sec of State for Health (Schering Ltd intervening)* [2002] in the High Court, and *R (Pretty) v DPP and Sec of State for Health* [2001] in the High Court and the House of Lords, among others. He is co-author of *Law and Medical Ethics,* writes for journals and media on medico-legal issues, has been a legal adviser to the General Optical Council, and has advised peers and MPs on related issues, including extensive drafting of bills and amendments.

Denise Charlesworth-Smith

Denise is a national campaigner for better end of life care, following the death of her father on the Liverpool Care Pathway (LCP). She was asked to attend the Round Table meeting by the Minister of State at the Department of Health in London (quoted in Hansard) and was then invited to be on Baroness Neuberger's Review Panel, which was tasked with reviewing the LCP and to propose recommendations for better end of life care. In 2013, the Panel produced its report, *More Care, Less Pathway: A Review of the Liverpool Care Pathway.*

She joined the Care Quality Commission as an 'expert by experience'. Her previous roles were in the police, insurance and local government. She has set up a support group for over 600 families who are facing the fallout of the problematic end of life care received by their loved ones.

Robert S. Harris

Robert S. Harris is a writer, researcher and editor. He has been a member of the Lords and Commons Family and Child Protection Group (LCFCPG) since 2011, and served as its Joint Convenor from 2014-2019. He led the Group's work in the production of *When 'End of Life Care' Goes Wrong.*

He has spoken at conferences and other events in Parliament and elsewhere, and has also been interviewed on radio and television. He is a fellow of the Royal Society of Arts, is a graduate in Philosophy from University College London and has a Graduate Diploma in Law from the College of Law (now the University of Law).

The Revd Lynda Rose

Lynda Rose is an Anglican priest and writer. Called to the Bar in 1983, she subsequently went into Christian ministry and was among the first women in the UK to be ordained into the Anglican Church. She served in parish ministry in and around Oxford for a number of years, but increasingly felt called to campaign on pro-life and related Christian issues. She is currently Director and CEO of **Voice for Justice UK** and Executive Director of **ParentPower**; she also serves as Convenor of the Lords and Commons Family and Child Protection Group, a non-aligned Parliamentary research group. She is the author of several books for both the religious and general markets.

When 'end of life care' goes wrong

Background

Sam H Ahmedzai, FRCP, Emeritus Professor

UK as a 'global leader' in end of life care

When 'end of life care' goes wrong is a surprising – perhaps shocking – title for a report to the British Parliament, for a topic in which many unquestioningly believe the United Kingdom is a world leader. Indeed, a search of the world literature on the development and standards of end of life care would show that the United Kingdom can safely call itself a global leader, both in terms of having the longest history of its incorporation into national healthcare and also by ratings from independent authorities.

One of most cited global rankings of end of life care, published in a white paper from the Economist Intelligence Unit (EIU) in 2015, placed the UK as overall number 1 just before Australia, out of 80 countries it surveyed and rated. (EIU, 2015) The UK also scored top in the categories of 'Palliative and healthcare environment', 'Quality of care' and equal first for 'Affordability of care'. It should be noted that to derive the rankings, the EIU "reviewed plans, policies and academic papers for each country, and conducted interviews with in-country professors, medical professionals and other experts.". Thus it should be noted that some of these parameters were more subjective than others.

I am a retired academic physician, specialised in palliative medicine, who has spent 30 years working in UK end of life care: the first nine spent in an independent charitable hospice and the following 21 years in an acute hospital trust and university. I am proud of the high standards of care I have seen given to people as they approach their end of life in the UK, not just in the specialist services where I was privileged to work, but in the community, and all kinds of hospital settings. But this Report is not for congratulating ourselves on our successes; rather, for taking a hard look at our weaknesses. The failings we have uncovered in the lived experience of patients and families are all the more disturbing, coming as they do from the 'leading country' in the world for end of life care.

Why this Report on UK end of life care?

So why have we produced this report on *When 'end of life care' goes wrong* in 2023? Surely there are more important areas of healthcare in which the UK is trailing, that need parliamentary attention? Our justification is simple: *listen to the people receiving end of life care, not just the 'experts'.*

One of the most dramatically informative public listening exercises performed in the UK healthcare arena occurred just under ten years ago. This was conducted by an independent Review Panel set up by Norman Lamb MP, then Minister of State for Community and Social Care, to be led by Baroness Julia Neuberger and which contained three lay members[1] out of a total of ten. The purpose of their review was to examine the nation's experience of an 'experiment' in end of life care which, from its inception in the late 1990s received first favourable, then mixed and finally derogatory feedback from the British public and some quarters of the professions.

The experiment was the endorsement by the Department of Health of the 'Liverpool Care Pathway' (LCP), which led to its sweeping adoption across the NHS – ultimately with the use of financial inducements to hospital trusts. The astonishing outcome of the review, published in 2013, were 44 recommendations - including for it to be abolished. (Liverpool Care Pathway Review Panel, 2013; see also Appendix 1 and Appendix 7). I use the word 'experiment' guardedly as it was a professionally driven implementation of an ideological vision about how people should die – but not a clinical trial as I, as an academic, would be expected to run prior to introducing a new medicine or healthcare technology.

Indeed, the first clinical trial of its use appeared in Italy after it had been abolished in the UK – and its results were mixed. Critically, most patients or family carers subjected to the LCP in the UK were not approached for informed consent before being placed on it, as we are also bound by medical ethics and regulatory bodies to do when trialling a new medical intervention.

Soon after the LCP was abolished, many national healthcare organisations (some of which, it must be said, had also previously endorsed and indeed promoted the LCP) gathered to form the 'Leadership Alliance for the Care of Dying People' (LACDP). This group, chaired by NHS England and having twenty four members including five lay representatives, published its own policy document and set of recommendations in 2014, by distilling from the LCP Review panel's 44 recommendations their own 'Five priorities for care'. (Leadership Alliance for the Care of Dying People, 2014; see also Appendix 2.)

The preface to the Leadership Alliance's five priorities read:

"The LCP was an approach to care developed during the 1990s, based on the care of the dying within the hospice setting, with the aim of transferring best practice to other settings. The review panel found evidence of both good and poor care delivered through use of the LCP and concluded that in some cases, the LCP had come to be regarded as a generic protocol and used as a tick box exercise. Generic protocols are not the right approach to caring for dying people: care should be individualised and reflect the needs and preferences of the dying person and those who are important to them" (See Appendix 2).

So how did end of life care in Britain come to such a drastic crisis and what difference has abolition of the LCP made in the past eight years? This chapter explores these two questions through a review of governmental and independent reports and policies, and by reflecting on the 16 patient and family case studies which form the core of this Report. These people had died between 2012 and 2021; they were aged from 21 to 94 (median 82) years. The informants who supplied their case studies were daughters and sons, parents, spouses. The deaths occurred in hospital (12), hospice care (4), care home (1). We thank these families – and many more who generously volunteered their experiences but are not included here for reason of space – for permission to share their stories.

What do we mean by 'end of life'?

First though, we should define the territory we are covering. In the 1960s - 70s, end of life care was hardly recognised in most countries' healthcare systems. But responding to the perceived pain and suffering of cancer patients, hospices had started to appear in Britain, followed soon in other parts of the world. What had rather harshly hitherto been called 'terminal care' became softened as 'hospice care'. But then, as now, less than 10% of British patients actually died in hospices: the large majority dying in hospitals, their own homes or increasingly over the decades, in care and nursing homes. So a new term emerged, which was initially welcomed and disputed in equal measure across the healthcare professions – 'palliative care'.[2]

The World Health Organisation (WHO) issued the world's first definition of palliative care in 1987, which has since gone through many revisions. Presently the WHO defines palliative care as: "an approach that improves the quality of life of patients (adults and children) and their families who are facing problems associated with life-threatening illness. It prevents and relieves suffering through the early identification, correct assessment and treatment of pain and other problems, whether physical, psychosocial, or spiritual." (WHO, 1987) It's more of a description, an aspiration than a definition – and certainly longwinded.

However, the subject of the present report is on 'end of life care' and that term appears to be even more difficult to define. This is largely because of the uncertainty of when 'end of life' begins and how long it could last.

The NHS defines it on its website by first repeating the WHO definition for palliative care and then, somewhat confusingly, adding "In England, the term 'end of life care' refers to the last year of life". Actually the NHS website for 'end of life care' is entitled 'Palliative and end of life care'. The timescale of end of life care in the NHS website's view is clearly about the remaining months, to year or so of life. (NHS Palliative and end of life care, 2022)

In contrast, the National Institute for Health and Care Excellence (NICE) produced its guidance NG31 in 2015 for "Care of dying adults in the last days of life", which "aims to improve end of life care for people in their last days of life". (NICE, 2015) To avoid any doubt, it adds: "adults (18 years and over) who are dying during the last 2 to 3 days of life". (see Appendix 3.)

Tackling head-on the conflicting messages about what 'end of life care' is, the NG31 guideline committee[3] stated that its remit "focused on care needed when a person is judged by the multi-professional clinical team to be within a few (2 to 3) days of death. This is different from other important NHS initiatives labelled 'end of life care' which are aimed at improving care for people in the last year or so of a chronic condition."

For the purposes of this Report, we are taking 'end of life care' to be aligned to NICE guidance NG31, namely when a person is thought to be in the last few days of life.

Why did the LCP often fail to deliver good care in the last days of life?

One reason for aligning with NG31 is that it was commissioned directly in the wake of the abolition of the Liverpool Care Pathway. Guideline NG31 started by summarising weaknesses of the LCP:

"There were 3 main areas of concern:

- recognising that a person was dying was not always supported by an experienced clinician and not reliably reviewed, even if the person may have had potential to improve

- the dying person may have been unduly sedated as a result of injudiciously prescribed symptom control medicines

- the perception that hydration and some essential medicines may have been withheld or withdrawn, resulting in a negative effect on the dying person.

These were not necessarily a direct consequence of following the LCP, but often happened because of poor or indiscriminate implementation and a lack of staff training and supervision." (NICE, 2015)

The writers of this Report are sad to share that these three areas of concern persist to this day and are repeatedly reflected in the following case studies. The first two deaths occurred during the time when the LCP was still being used, but the rest describe deaths after its abolition, right up to 2021.

Another 'existential' weakness in the ethos of the LCP was that it was based on the notion of a 'good death' as provided by many UK charitable hospices in the 1990s, which were then working largely outside of the NHS with highly trained specialist doctors and nurses, and often a higher staff to patient ratio than prevailed in the NHS. Implementing such a model without prior formal testing in busy NHS locations, especially with limited training of staff who are often conflicted by their duties for life-saving care, was surely going to be problematic (for a more recent critique of the LCP, including how NHS financial incentives were controversially offered before 2013 to hospitals for using it, see Appendix 7).

Thus an important message from NICE guideline NG31 was that it should be applied to all settings in which NHS care was given, including hospitals, hospices, care and nursing homes, patients' homes, prisons etc. (See Appendix 3 for more on NG31's brief.)

NHS guidance on end of life care before and after abolition of the LCP

It will be clear from the case studies presented in the next section that 9 years after the LCP review panel's 44 recommendations, and subsequently the Leadership Alliance for the Care of Dying People's 5 priorities for care and NICE NG31 guidance's 72 recommendations, care of dying people in their last days of life in the UK may still fall short of their expectations. We found that these failings appear in hospitals, hospices, care homes and people's own homes. The case studies are all distressing to read in different ways, but one thing that unites them is the failure to personalise care, by applying a one-size fits all, tick-box approach that was the hallmark of the LCP where it was poorly implemented.

Thus in many of our case studies, patients and their family members in a range of settings were experiencing an end of life care pathway which was similar to the LCP in all but name (see case studies 3, 5, 6, 7, 9, 10, 11, 12, 15, 16). Some families had even challenged health professionals as to whether the LCP was being used with their relative after 2014 (see case studies 5, 9). This was met with a denial, but on studying the evidence supplied, I could see that some of the negative practices of the LCP were still being applied.

Even before the abolition of the LCP and the subsequent NHS guidelines, as early as 2010 the General Medical Council (GMC) had issued directions to medical practitioners on 'Treatment and care towards the end of life: good practice in decision making". (GMC, 2010)

This GMC guidance to doctors is prefaced with:

"Patients coming to the end of their lives need high quality care and treatment. Providing this care is likely to involve making difficult and emotionally challenging decisions. This guidance provides you with a framework to support you in meeting the needs of your patient as they come towards the end of their life."

(See Appendix 4 for more extracts from the GMC guidance to doctors.)

The GMC guidance goes on to describe scenarios where doctors need to be aware of these needs, including when patients lack mental capacity, the provision of nutrition and hydration, and handling cardiopulmonary resuscitation (CPR) decisions. These topics will be explored in more detail in some of the case studies. It should be noted that the GMC viewed end of life care to apply not only to patients with chronic progressive illness such as cancer or dementia, but also to those with sudden life-threatening health crises.

GMC guidance is specifically for registered doctors, while other NHS guidance, including NICE guidelines, apply to all health and social care professionals. For example, the LCP Review panel recognised that nurses also contributed to poor practice under the LCP, recommending:

"13. As a matter of urgency the Nursing and Midwifery Council should Issue for nurses guidance on good practice in decision-making in end of life care, equivalent to that issued by the General Medical Council for doctors."

(For all LCP Review panel recommendations for nursing, see case studies 7, 16, 34 and 41 in Appendix 1).

Some of the case studies we review have examples of where the nursing role in the last days of life was unacceptable (for example, see case studies 3, 5, 7, 9, 10, 11, 13, 15, 16.)

In which scenarios are people still being failed at end of life?

NICE guideline NG31 identified these areas for improving care in the last days:

"This guideline provides recommendations to help healthcare professionals to recognize when a person is entering the last days of life or may have stabilized or be improving even temporarily; to communicate and share decisions respectfully with the dying person and people important to them; and to manage hydration and commonly experienced symptoms to maintain the person's comfort and dignity without causing unacceptable side effects." (See Appendix 3.)

We found many distressing experiences which arose from health professionals' failure to follow either, or both NICE and GMC guidance on these scenarios.

Recognising dying – and the possibility of recovery

The LCP Review panel identified a recurring problem when patients were inappropriately identified as 'dying'. Our case studies show examples where patients are still being treated as if they were at the end of life, but without a proper assessment of being near to 'dying' by suitably experienced staff. In other cases, patients may have been potentially dying at first assessment, but then stabilised or had the capacity to improve, and yet continued to be managed as if they were still near to death. (See for example, case studies 3, 6, 7, 8, 10,)

Supporting hydration and nutrition at the end of life

The GMC's 2010 guidance to all registered practising doctors was clear on the importance of listening to patients and those important to them, about supporting hydration including the use of 'clinically assisted hydration'. (See Appendix 4; and the Compendium of Terms for explanation of 'Nutrition and hydration.)

Yet a scenario we commonly observed was when hydration and sometimes nutrition were withdrawn or withheld, if the clinical team thought they were at the end of life – even against the wishes of patients and families. (See case studies 4, 5, 6, 7, 8, 9, 10, 11, 15, 16) Again, this was one of the abhorrent aspects of the rigid 'one-size-fits-all' approach to using the LCP that the Review panel condemned.

NICE guideline NG31 also specifically addressed this issue with no less than 10 recommendations, such as:

"1.4.1 Support the dying person to drink if they wish to and are able to. Check for any difficulties, such as swallowing problems or risk of aspiration. Discuss the risks and benefits of continuing to drink, with the dying person, and those involved in the dying person's care."

(See Appendix 3 for more on this topic.)

Decision-making about cardiopulmonary resuscitation (CPR)

Many of our case study informants found (sometimes after the death) that their relative had been placed unilaterally by healthcare professionals on a 'Do not attempt CPR' or DNACPR order. (See the Compendium of terms for explanation of these and other terms.) Strictly speaking doctors do not need permission to withhold CPR if it is considered futile or harmful. What they cannot do is impose CPR if the patient wishes against it.

In many of the case studies, the fear some families had was that agreeing to a DNACPR order would lead to the automatic withholding of other life supporting or even comfort measures, such as giving food and fluids, or antibiotics (see case studies 3, 10). In two cases, it is my medical opinion that patients had been placed wrongly on a DNACPR order; their life may have been prolonged if they had opportunity to have CPR (case studies, 13, 14).

GMC (2010) guidance covers CPR decisions very clearly, but still patients and families are being distressed because of poor communication and the lack of shared decision-making on these issues. A recent option published in 2020 is the ReSPECT process, in which decisions about CPR are made with the patient alongside other forms of supportive care and treatment (Hawkes et al, 2020; see also Appendix 8.) However, even this requires doctors to make time and opportunity - and have training - to have these discussions, which for these reasons are frequently not happening. (See also case studies 3, 9, 10, 12.)

Mental capacity

As people are dying, especially those who are older, they may lose capacity to make key decisions about their health. NICE guideline NG31 (2015) acknowledged this: "For some people who are entering the last days of life, mental capacity to understand and engage in shared decision-making may be limited. This could be temporary or fluctuating, for example it may be caused by delirium associated with an infection or a biochemical imbalance such as dehydration or organ failure, or it could be a permanent loss of capacity from dementia or other similar irreversible conditions" (see Appendix 3).

The Mental Capacity Act (2005) set out a clear framework for assessment of mental capacity and how lack of it should be dealt with in critical decision-making about health as well as living wills. (Mental Capacity Act 2005)

GMC guidance went to lengths to inform doctors of their duties for patients who lacked mental capacity in relation to end of life decisions and plans. (See Appendix 4) Yet we have seen disturbing case studies where doctors failed to take mental capacity into account when making decisions about starting or withholding treatments, including not consulting with relatives who held lasting power of attorney. (See case studies 2, 7, 8, 10, 12, 13, 14.)

The most shocking example of this failing was case study 7, which concerned a young lady of 21 who had severe learning disabilities. She went into hospital in 2016 for a routine minor operation but died after three and a half weeks; the coroner's inquest found that malnutrition contributed to her death. Her parents had begged daily for her to be fed, yet the medical team failed to hold a 'Best Interests' meeting, which the coroner found to be unlawful.

Effect of the Covid-19 pandemic

The people in our case studies had died between 2012 till 2021. The COVID-19 pandemic affected the UK from the beginning of 2020 and four of the deaths occurred during it (case studies 13-16). The families report difficulties in visiting or staying with dying relatives, which we know was a widespread problem across healthcare, causing great distress in the past 3 years. But we found no evidence that the pandemic had any other direct influence on how these people had died.

There have been reports that during the pandemic there was an increase in DNACPR orders being placed in elderly residents of care homes, often without their knowledge; this was condemned by families and the media.[4] (CQC, 2020) Out of the four cases we gathered from the 'pandemic' time, one (case study 14) concerned a 47 year old man dying in hospital who had a DNACPR order placed on him, without his or his daughter's knowledge. I can argue that having CPR might have made a difference to his outcome. But whether this can be attributed to the pandemic, or underlying poor medical practice, is debatable.

Health and Care Act 2022

We are aware that while this Report was being prepared, the Health and Care Act 2022 was passed by Parliament. The original Bill included an amendment about palliative care proposed by Baroness Professor Finlay, a palliative care professional herself; however this was withdrawn. The Government's final and accepted amendment was less extensive than Baroness Finlay's, but still has ensured the responsibility of all healthcare commissioners to provide specialist palliative care in every NHS setting. (See Appendix 9, which also contains an extract from subsequent NHS Statutory Guidance for Integrated Care Boards, issued July 2022.)

We warmly welcome this amendment which should have a very positive effect in making access to specialist palliative care more equitable across the UK. However, we should point out that since four of the deaths we cover actually occurred in hospice care (which are, by definition, settings of specialist palliative care), it is unclear to us how much impact the new Act will have on the poor communication we have observed between patients, family and staff, or on the delivery of suboptimal or frankly negligent practices in all settings. (See case studies 6, 11, 13, 15.)

Moreover, many of what we believe to be indefensible end of life decisions in other cases were made unilaterally by general clinicians with patients who were not thought to be terminally ill, but having acute medical crises which could end in death. As mentioned at the beginning of this Background, this category was declared by GMC (2010) guidance as also being an 'end of life' scenario, but these patients may never have come under the purview of 'specialist palliative care' services at all. (See case studies 2 (ICU setting), 3 (A&E), 4 (geriatric department), 5 (general medicine), 7 (infectious diseases unit and ICU), 8 (post-operative recovery), 10 (acute hospital), 12 (A&E), 14 (A&E, renal department), 16 (general medicine)). Thus we believe that this Report to Parliamentarians will highlight the need for extra vigilance for patients in all settings, which may lie beyond the provision of the new Act.

Next section – Case Studies

This Introduction has referred many times to the 16 case studies we received and have incorporated into the next section of this Report. It may be helpful to clarify when these deaths arose with respect to the LCP and official guidance on end of life following its abolition.

Case studies 1 and 2 arose during the time that the LCP was in regular practice. Case study 3 occurred in the interim period between the announcement of the abolition of the LCP and its final removal, but was covered by the published LCP Review panel's recommendations and the Five Priorities for Care; case studies 4 and 5 occurred after the LCP was abolished but before the NICE guidance NG31 was published; all later case studies were covered by NICE NG31. In addition, it is important to know that the GMC guidance (2010) was extant throughout and this issued – to registered doctors – very detailed recommendations on many of the issues covered in this Report.

My role as a former consultant physician working in end of life care for 30 years is to express my personal opinions on medical, ethical, and – where I can – legal implications of the cases. Thus after each statement about the person who died, I have written my 'medical opinion'. These are entirely my personal professional judgements and do not necessarily represent the views of the Lords and Commons Family and Child Protection Group.

Following the next chapter, the concluding chapter will contain personal observations and opinions from James Bogle, a barrister with long experience in end of life cases, citing authority on the legal implications of the cases.

---

[1] Declaration of Interest: Denise Charlesworth-Smith, co-author of this Report, was one of the three lay members of the LCP Review panel.

[2] There is no space here to discuss the interesting etymology of 'palliative' and why it changed from signifying the mere relieving of symptoms of illness in any area of medicine in general, to embrace the holistic care of people approaching the end of life, in particular. Nor moreover, why a group of professionals emerging in the 1980s came to adopt this term as a badge of their specialty.

[3] Declaration of interest: I was the chair of the committee which produced NICE guideline NG31.

[4] *Blanket 'do not resuscitate' orders imposed on English care homes, finds CQC*. The Guardian, 18 March 2021. https://www.theguardian.com/society/2021/mar/18/blanket-do-not-resuscitate-orders-imposed-on-english-care-homes-finds-cqc

WHEN 'END OF LIFE CARE' GOES WRONG

16
CASE STUDIES

Table of demographic and geographic distribution of case studies

Case Study	Year of death	Gender	Age	Place of Death	Country	City / County	Relationship of informant
1	2012	Male	82	Hospital	England	Sutton-in-Ashfield, Nottinghamshire	Father
2	2012	Male	68	Hospital	England	Liverpool	Father
3	2014	Male	78	Hospital	England	Chester	Husband
4	2015	Female	86	Hospital	England	Canterbury	Mother
5	2015	Female	82	Hospital	England	Stoke on Trent	Mother
6	2016	Female	88	Hospice at Home	England	Harrow, Middlesex	Mother
7	2016	Female	21	Hospital	England	Sheffield	Daughter
8	2017	Female	86	Hospital	England	Hull	Mother
9	2017	Male	52	Hospice	Wales	Cardiff	Husband
10a	2017	Male	88	Hospital	Wales	Cardiff	Mother
10b	2021	Female	92	Hospital	Wales	Cardiff	Father
11	2018	Male	61	Hospice	England	Milton Keynes	Husband
12	2018	Female	94	Hospital	England	Wigan	Mother
13	2020	Male	89	Care Home	England	Carlisle	Father
14	2020	Male	47	Hospital	England	Manchester	Father
15	2021	Female	73	Hospice at Home	England	Ivybridge, Devon	Mother
16	2021	Male	84	Hospital	England	Northallerton, North Yorkshire	Father

This Report is based on the experiences of sixteen families.

However, in one case (No. 10), a daughter supplied information on the deaths of both her parents, which brings the total number of deceased to seventeen.

The case studies cover the deaths of nine males and eight females. These deaths occurred between 2012 and 2021.

The first two deaths occurred while the Liverpool Care Pathway (LCP) was in use;

the third occurred in the interval between the LCP Review panel calling for the abolition and the final date of abolition in mid-2014;

the next two occurred in the period between the abolition of the LCP and the publication of NICE NG31 guideline in December 2015;

and the remaining eleven deaths were covered by NG31.

The ages of the decedents ranged from 21 years to 94, with an average age of 74.8 years.

Twelve of the deaths occurred in hospitals;

two as in-patients in hospices;

two under hospice at home care; and one in a care home.

Information for the case studies were supplied by the decedents' daughters (13 deaths); sons (3 deaths); and parents (1 death).

Fourteen of the deaths occurred in England, three in Wales.

WHEN 'END OF LIFE CARE' GOES WRONG

CASE STUDY 1

My background

My father was a victim of the Liverpool Care Pathway, leading to an avoidable death, committed by a junior doctor, with four months' experience, acting alone during a night shift. He was put on a syringe driver, sedated and euthanised by the use of midazolam and morphine. On the medical certificate for the cause of death, it stated in one of the sections that my dad died as a result of the LCP as cited on the death certificate. As a family we did not know what this meant, so I started asking questions, as I needed help to justify what had happened. I had to speak up about this and had an opportunity to speak with Sir Norman Lamb (the then coalition Care Minister). I was invited by him to sit on Baroness Neuberger's panel, *More Care, Less Pathway*.[1] Included among the ten panel members, there were Lords Guthrie, Hameed and Harries, and leaders from the nursing, medical, legal and charitable sectors.

The Neuberger Panel sought views from families who had lost loved ones, where the deaths had been avoidable, and spoke to Professor John Ellershaw, who had developed the Liverpool Care Pathway, telling him about these deaths.

Recommendations of the Neuberger Review

600 families have contacted me for help via the support group I created in 2018. My discussions with them show that the Neuberger recommendations (of which there were 44 in total) for changes after the LCP are failing:

1) Personalised end of life care plans are not being discussed, while many families are unaware that the patient is even dying, let alone unwell;

2) Junior doctors are often the only available clinician making decisions, raising concerns about "a general principle that a patient should only be placed on end of life care by a senior responsible clinician";

3) NICE guidance on end of life care not being adhered to en bloc, a concern that I have raised with them;

4) Despite guidance issued by the Nursing and Midwifery Council, this is not followed through by trained or compassionate nurses, possibly due to incorrect staffing on the wards, burn-out and absence of senior

nurses/ward managers;

5) Quality of care for the dying has become worse:

- families are not being consulted, blanket DNARs are put on loved ones (even prior to COVID);

- loved ones refused food and fluid, often Nil by Mouth for a number of days, leading to patients becoming malnourished and dehydrated, leading to pain for which they are then sedated or sedated without explanation. The method of dealing with patients has been appalling.

These observations, made following discussions with families as a result of being ignored by Matt Hancock, the previous Health and Social Care Secretary, led to a forum being held where families travelled from across the UK to discuss their concerns and present their evidence to me. I set up a support group in June 2018 which is rapidly growing in numbers.

Nothing has changed since the Neuberger panel last met and the chair of the report called 'One Chance to Get it Right' produced by a multiprofessional group after the fall of the LCP, is failing to engage with me, despite me contacting her several times since 2018 when the number of cases was rising.

My work on a Care Quality Commission (CQC) Inspection Team

After the panel completed its work in 2013, I joined a CQC inspection team, trained as an Expert by Experience. The CQC failed to take on board my concerns about end of life care and I resigned. I was concerned that the inspection team failed to notice on arrival that patients were not being cared for properly. Even though I made the team aware of this, I was extremely concerned to find that the institution we visited would nonetheless receive a good rating. It made no sense.

Contact with stakeholders

I raised the need to re-address the concerns I had with the previous Health and Social Care Secretary, via the former Care Minister who was responsible for the review. Whilst Sir Norman was incredibly supportive, I received no acknowledgement email from the Health and Social Care Secretary when Sir Norman wrote to him in 2018, despite sending him details of what was happening in his constituency. I have also written to the head of NHS

England with no response. Sir Norman Lamb has kept a watching brief over what has been happening and I regularly discuss what is happening with him. He has now put pressure on the National Clinical Director for End of Life Care (and chair of the 2014 One Chance to Get it Right panel), Professor Bee Wee, for a response too, but to date she has twice stated a need to discuss with colleagues but fails to provide any response to me.

Medical opinion of Professor Ahmedzai

1. This case study is qualitatively different from the others which follow in this Report, in three respects. First, it starts with a case history of a man who died not only during the period when the Liverpool Care Pathway (LCP) was being used in UK hospitals, but actually is certified as dying in accordance with it. The latter in itself is noteworthy, because the LCP is not a recognised medical condition or precursor to one, that could cause death. Rather, it was meant to represent a protocol or pathway for making deaths more comfortable. The observation that the LCP had been invoked during the night by a single newly qualified junior doctor adds all the more to the pathos of, what we are told, was a potentially avoidable death.

As the independent Neuberger LCP Review Panel found in its 2013 report, there were numerous case histories like this which showed that the LCP was being used frequently as a "tick-box" exercise. This means it was allowing inexperienced and unsupported staff, who were not trained to recognise when someone was dying or could potentially recover, to make life-or-death decisions and act on them with powerful drugs that could indeed, in some cases, accelerate death.

A further critique of the LCP was that it enabled "blanket" prescriptions of several drugs which individually could play a part in relieving one or other symptom of a dying person, but by being all written on a chart together, meant that inevitably often they were given together in a blanket fashion.

2. Second, this case study invokes two key actions that arose after the government set up the independent Review Panel chaired by Baroness Julia Neuberger, that reported on these and other failings of the LCP in mid-2013. [As Denise Charlesworth-Smith, the author of this case study declares, she herself was a national campaigner on the Neuberger Review Panel; and she is one of the contributors of this Report.]

The first was a document produced by a multi-professional panel of health and care leaders and experts, led by the National Clinical Director for End of Life Care, Professsor Bee Wee, that attempted to distil the key lessons learnt from the Neuberger Review Panel's 44 recommendations into a set of five 'Priorities for Care' of dying people. These were published in a report called 'One Chance to Get it Right' in 2014. Interestingly, out of the 23 members of this panel who between them represented 25 professional organisations (who called themselves the 'Leadership Alliance'), it appears not one was from a patient or public representative body.

The second action was the commissioning of a new national guideline from NICE on end of life care, to offer clinicians robust guidance after the withdrawal of the LCP. This led to the NICE guideline NG31 'Care of the Dying Adult in the Last Days of Life', published in 2015 (see Appendix 3).[2] NICE has a strict policy of having patient and carer representation on its guideline development groups. NG31 gave the first set of evidence-based guidelines to be followed wherever patients were receiving care from the NHS – whether in hospitals, at home, in nursing or care homes or in hospices.

The recommendations from the Neuberger LCP review panel (see Appendix 1), from 'One Chance to Get it Right' (see Appendix 2), and NICE NG31 (see Appendix 3) – as well as relevant guidance from professional bodies such as the General Medical Council (see Appendix 4) – will be cited frequently in the discussion of the following case studies found in this current Report.

3. Third, the current case study describes the support group set up by its author in the wake of her concerns following her perceived lack of progress after the LCP Review Panel, the 'One Chance to Get it Right' report and even the NICE NG31 guideline. In addition, her spell as a CQC inspector showed her how even this national monitoring body could fail to detect failures of hospitals to change their practices, many years after the abolition of the LCP.

4. With this "scene-setting" case study, there follow 15 other case studies with more detailed accounts of disturbing and even harrowing experiences of patients and families in end of life care as it is practiced across the UK. After each case study, I will add my expert clinical opinion about the quality of care given and on what the stories tell us about current NHS end of life care.

---

[1] *More Care, Less Pathway: A Review of the Liverpool Care Pathway*, July 2013. https://assets.publishing.service.gov.uk/government/uploads/system/uploads/attachment_data/file/212450/

[2] Declaration of interest: Sam H Ahmedzai who chaired the development of NICE guideline NG31 is one of the contributors to this Report.

WHEN 'END OF LIFE CARE' GOES WRONG

CASE STUDY 2

Editor's note:

Except for Case Studies 1 and 2, all subsequent Case Studies in this Report draw on the post-LCP period. Case Study 2, which saw the family take their case to the Supreme Court, is included here to help provide essential background to some of the issues regarding end of life care, as they existed shortly before the LCP was abolished.

Background

My family's story began when my father was admitted to Aintree Hospital with abdominal pain in 2012. After initial tests were carried out, a diagnosis of constipation was given and doctors advised that Dad remain in hospital so they could administer medication until his bowel function resumed. Unfortunately, Dad acquired an infection in hospital, developing into hospital-acquired pneumonia and sepsis, resulting in him becoming critically ill and being admitted into the critical care unit (CCU) after just three weeks in the care of the hospital.

Doctors communicated their prognosis of Dad's rapid deterioration as septic shock, dehydration and organ failure, saying that treatments were futile. They wanted us to agree for them to withdraw all treatments.

Challenging doctors on withdrawing treatments: Liverpool Care Pathway and Best Interests meetings

Doctors were not fully communicating with the family regarding factors which led up to my father's rapid deterioration, so we could not agree with them stopping the treatments.

Although doctors were telling us Dad was dying and treatments were futile, he actually lived a further seven months on CCU. Dad was progressing and responding to treatments, to the point of a rehabilitation plan being put in place for him to come home. Unfortunately, Dad caught numerous infections in the hospital, which would set him back, resulting in numerous Best Interests meetings with doctors over several months. All of these proved unsuccessful, as the family were not being fully informed, so a mutual decision could not be reached regarding withdrawing treatments.

Court of Protection and Appeals Court

As a decision was not agreed between the family and doctors, the hospital started legal proceedings in the Court of Protection, seeking a declaration to make it lawful to withdraw treatments for Dad. The case went to trial in the High Court, which the family won with overwhelming evidence. It was ruled that treatments were not futile, that Dad had a "life worth living" and that treatments should continue.

The hospital appealed the decision when Dad caught another infection in December 2012. The declaration to withdraw treatment was sought and this was upheld by the Court. Sadly, my Dad died on December 31st 2012.

Supreme Court ruling [1]

My family took the case to the Supreme Court in 2013, as there was a conflict in the law between rulings in the Court of Protection and the Appeal Court. Solicitors acting for the family stated: "The Court of Appeal was wrong both to find life-prolonging treatments futile and that he had no prospect of recovery". The finding that the Court of Appeal was wrong in its reasoning justified taking the case to the Supreme Court, as Dad "would have wished doctors to prolong his life". The Court set down important principles for those caring for critically ill patients.

It has been said of this case:

"Perhaps the most significant element of this judgment is the weight placed on the role of the patient's (or their family's) wishes in determining what constitutes a worthwhile recovery, and what is in their best interests. Lady Hale's exposition of this will be relevant to patients with capacity as well as those, like here, whose interests [fail] to be considered under the Mental Capacity Act. It sets out a clear imperative for participation and consultation with patients and their families in making sensitive decisions about their future healthcare." [2]

Some highlights of Lady Hale's lead judgment are:

'The authorities are all agreed that the starting point is a strong presumption that it is in a person's best interests to stay alive. As Sir Thomas Bingham MR said in the Court of Appeal in Bland ... "A profound respect for the sanctity of human life is embedded in our law and our moral philosophy".' [3]

"... that in considering the best interests of this particular patient at this particular time, decision-makers must look at his welfare in the widest sense, not just medical but social and psychological; they must consider the nature of the medical treatment in question, what it involves and its prospects of success; they must consider what the outcome of that treatment for the patient is likely to be; they must try and put themselves in the place of the individual patient and ask what his attitude to the treatment is or would be likely to be; and they must consult others who are looking after him or interested in his welfare, in particular for their view of what his attitude would be." [4]

"[As part of] the patient's welfare... great weight [had] to be given to Mr James' family life which was "of the closest and most meaningful kind". [5]

Formal NHS complaint

The family still seek answers today regarding what happened to Dad in the hospital's care, in the form of a hospital complaint, contacting the NHS Ombudsman, meetings with the CQC and our local MP, FOI and subject access requests. All remain unsuccessful in answering our questions for closure.

Medical opinion of Professor Ahmedzai

This is a most remarkable medical case with such a prolonged stay in CCU, which before the COVID-19 pandemic was probably unique. Having read supplementary documents about this case, I can see that the hospital staff had been treating him intensively, including the use of cardiopulmonary resuscitation (CPR), for various infections and instances of organ failure.

1. The relevance of this case lies in the change in attitude of the hospital medical team, who came to the view that offering supportive and invasive treatments would no longer be in the patient's best interests. The subsequent High Court hearing and appeal against its initial judgement show how hard it is to make decisions in the best interests of a person who has lost capacity to make medical decisions, and who is facing life-threatening complications.

2. The first significance of the final Supreme Court judgement is that it made very clear statements about how "best interests" decisions should be made in such cases, and what tests should apply in judging, for example, what is meant by a "futile" treatment.

3. Third, it emphasised the need to consider the patient in the context of the family who is supporting the patient in these extreme circumstances. My understanding of the legal position of family members is that in the consideration of 'best interests', only those who have been granted by the patient to have Lasting Power of Attorney for such decisions, can – and must – have their contribution to the decision-making.

4. My final observation is that I am at a loss to understand how the family has not received satisfactory responses to the FOIs and other actions over the past nine years since Mr James' death. To me this shows that current systems in the NHS are not geared well towards resolving difficult disputes concerning end of life decision-making in a timely manner, bearing in mind the psychological trauma borne by those bereaved.

---

[1] https://www.supremecourt.uk/cases/docs/uksc-2013-0134-judgment.pdf

[2] http://ukscblog.com/case-comment-aintree-university-hospitals-nhs-foundation-trust-v-james-2013-uksc-67/

[3] Para 35.

[4] Para 39.

[5] Para 40.

CASE STUDY 3

Background

John's medical history was complex and detailed. At the time of his death, he suffered principally from COPD (chronic obstructive pulmonary disease) and AF (atrial fibrillation) with heart failure. Lung cancer had meant the removal of a complete lung in 1986. John had oxygen at home.

In 2013 John's legs, ankles and feet were swollen, affecting his mobility. He sat with his legs on a pillow, on a footstool. Three GPs declined our repeated pleas for referrals and only treated the superficial symptoms of the increasingly frequent "flare-ups". Our community matron was replaced by a woman appointed as community matron, yet later it emerged that she was an occupational therapist, with no nursing qualifications or training. Our request for help from the respiratory physiotherapist also fell upon deaf ears.

In November 2013, a visit to the health centre resulted in the practice manager arranging a home visit from the GP – who looked at John and referred him there and then. John was acutely unwell over Christmas. He was admitted to the Countess of Chester Hospital on 28th December and discharged on 4th January.

On 7th January, John was very unwell. A GP attended at 1.25pm and said he'd never seen John look so ill, and that he was going back to the surgery to arrange for an ambulance. No ambulance arrived, until I rang the surgery at 4pm, and was advised to ring 999. Upon arrival, the paramedics asked why the GP had not rung for an ambulance whilst he was here. John had respiratory failure upon insertion of a cannula, but was resuscitated in the ambulance.

After a lengthy wait in the relatives' room of the resuscitation area in the hospital with my granddaughter and my son-in-law, one of the paramedics told us that John was "okay", that he had independent respiratory and cardiac output, and that he was waiting to be assessed for ICU (intensive care units). The consultant came in and told us that they were leaving John to "slip away naturally". I told him what the paramedic had said, and he was clearly not pleased. He repeated his earlier comment and I replied "No, I want you to do the very best you can for him please".

We entered the resuscitation room to see John. My son-in-law preceded me and was greeted in the usual way. I saw that John was not attached to any machinery. I asked him if he had any pain, and he said "No". We were talking to him, though he was a little breathless, which was normal for him. A nurse in a striped dress (bearing no name-badge) came up behind him and slipped a tube into his nostril without telling him, and she just ignored me when I said "Hello". John was saying that we had had a lousy Christmas, but we would have a better one next year. As he was speaking, the blonde woman who had earlier entered the relatives' room with the consultant walked in. It was inconceivable that she did not hear John talking. She too was bearing no name-badge.

Injection without explanation

She walked around the table, picked up John's arm and gave him an injection without explaining to him what it was for. She dropped his arm back onto the bed and walked out. She had not spoken to us or acknowledged our presence in any way. None of us had seen that she had a syringe in her hand. Thirty seconds later, John died. Upon leaving the room to tell our family and friends, a young woman asked if they could "have his skin". Again, she wore no name-badge.

We were told by another nurse – who called down the corridor to us – that we couldn't leave, as a police officer was on the way to ID John's body. There was no inquest or autopsy. Once this was done, we waited around a little, but no-one came, so we went home. The GP signed the death certificate.

Events after John's death

In 2015 I was informed by letter that John had been given morphine and midazolam, ostensibly because he was "agitated and in pain". There were multiple warnings of morphine intolerance in John's medical records.

After my father's death, I telephoned the Coroner, who told me that John's death was not due to natural causes. I was advised to contact the police. Despite being told by a detective constable that they were "looking at" involuntary manslaughter and that had John's body not been cremated, they would have applied for an exhumation order, the investigation – such as it was – was closed as there was no histology.

The two names used by the person who administered the injection were not on the GMC database as a "qualified clinician". The consultant informed the Chief Coroner that John was given midazolam. The last firm of solicitors I had consulted confirmed in writing in 2018 that this was a criminal matter. It was at this point that the fabricated and falsified DNR note appeared. It claimed that my consent had been obtained not to resuscitate John. This document is signed by a doctor who we did not meet at any point on the evening of John's death. Most worryingly, Cheshire CID accepted it as genuine.

A medical examiner wrote and told me that the Coroner's decision not to hold an inquest should have been judicially reviewed. In a letter from a barrister, I was told that the police did not need histology, and that he could not see how an inquest jury could fail to bring in a verdict of unlawful killing.

There was never, at any time, any terminal diagnosis.

Medical opinion of Professor Ahmedzai

1. This is a very distressing case, on account of many key features. First, it appears that an older person with multiple co-morbidities had apparently been allowed to deteriorate over months at home without appropriate specialist cardiac and respiratory care; and even when he was seen at home on this last day there was a three-hour delay in arranging an ambulance. Had he received specialist community nursing assessments at home and been brought to hospital earlier, in my opinion on the balance of probabilities, the outcome on 7th January 2014 could have been different.

2. Second, the family's statement of events that befell Mr Williams and his family on 7th January 2014, from 12.45pm when a GP first called at his home until he was certified as dead in the hospital at 7.16pm, is very distressing to read. I have had the benefit of reviewing several supplementary documents related to Mr Williams' last day, and in particular I refer to a detailed medical summary from the consultant in emergency medicine at the hospital, and letters from the Coroner in 2017.

There was a delay of three hours between the first GP seeing him (who failed to call an ambulance as he had said he would) and the ambulance arriving after the family's 999 call. The paramedic who attended Mr Williams had recorded a "pre-hospital cardiac arrest" while he was being moved from the house to ambulance. He was given cardiopulmonary resuscitation (CPR) successfully with two cycles of electric shocks and his heart and circulation restarted.

On arrival at the hospital, he was found to require assistance with breathing, and so he had a tube inserted into his windpipe for a ventilator for this purpose. He had type 2 respiratory failure, which occurs when not only is the blood oxygen low, but the carbon dioxide content is also high. He was clearly gravely ill and according to the records I have seen, he received rapid and standard medical support in the form of intravenous drugs and ventilation.

The emergency department consultant has written that the view of the attending team was that owing to his very poor current medical condition and his numerous previous chronic conditions, it was thought unlikely he would benefit from an admission to the intensive care unit (ICU) and "recover with a reasonable quality of life". Apparently two doctors spoke with the family and explained his poor prognosis and their decision making. A senior anaesthetist was consulted who agreed with the decision not to admit to ICU. The hospital consultant stated that a "DNACPR was completed with agreement from the family".

The tube for mechanical ventilation was removed and normal practice in this scenario would be to continue supplying oxygen. From the daughter's statement, it would appear that she witnessed nasal tubes being inserted for this purpose. She also informs us that he was still able to converse "though he was a little breathless, which was normal for him". She also states, "I asked him if he had any pain, and he said "No". Thus from her direct observations, he was neither in pain nor distressed or agitated.

The emergency department consultant's letter confirmed that around this time one of the doctors administered an injection of 1mg morphine together with 1mg midazolam. Mr Williams would most likely have lost the capacity to breathe spontaneously very soon afterwards. The doctor's letter actually referred to this injection three times. First, "[a doctor] administered a small dose of morphine (1mg) and midazolam (1mg) to treat agitation and distress". Second, "I feel that the administration of the midazolam and morphine is appropriate for a patient in distress as it will help reduce their agitation and pain".

The actual doses given were very small (1mg of each) but nevertheless pharmacologically active, and together in a person known to have type 2 respiratory failure, they could, from my experience, have contributed to the cessation of his breathing. I am bound to say that while it is understandable that Mr Williams would be distressed and possibly agitated during this admission — and predictably these would increase immediately after extubation (removal of the ventilation tube) — I could see no evidence that he had pain. His daughter specifically denies that he had pain and the conversation they had about the weather suggests he was probably not too agitated.

My understanding is that the co-administration of both morphine and midazolam was possibly part of a protocol used in ICUs to calm patients who were having mechanical ventilation removed. Midazolam is an effective sedative for the distress that may follow extubation, and could have been used alone. However, in my opinion, the addition of morphine at this time was probably redundant. Morphine is a very powerful respiratory depressant and it is possible that if he had received only small repeated doses of midazolam, he would have still stopped breathing eventually but not so rapidly, which would have allowed the family more time to be with him.

The third mention in the consultant's letter of this injection was in a list of drugs given to Mr Williams with their exact timings. Here, he stated "I am unable to ascertain the exact time that the morphine and midazolam were given from the records." I find it extraordinary that five doses of three other drugs were documented with exact times, but not the giving of morphine and midazolam. My inference is that within the team, there was a realisation that the co-administration of these drugs was directly responsible for the cessation of breathing and this had been witnessed by the family: "Thirty seconds later, John died." And yet they have inexplicably "lost" the timing of this last injection.

My reflection on this sequence of events, which I have described in detail to explain the "medical side" of what the Williams family was experiencing, has two strands. First, it is my opinion that from what I have seen, the medical management of Mr Williams in the hospital until the time of the decision to withdraw ventilation was appropriate, timely and standard practice. However, I believe that the communication of how these decisions were made, and the involvement of the family in this rapidly changing situation, left a lot to be desired. Specifically, the family were made to witness what they could only interpret as an act of involuntary "euthanasia" — the medical acceleration of death in a dying person. The hospital's denying the timing of the final injection would seem, in the circumstances, to support their guilt in this.

I have read that the doctor who administered the injection was a trainee anaesthetist. Although the medical act may have been justifiable, the family's description of this staff member's silence and even failure to acknowledge the family's presence in the final minutes of Mr Williams' life seems to be callous and inhumane in the extreme.

Other aspects of the family's recollections confirm that although the care may have been medically "correct", the attention to their human needs was lacking, for example being told to stay with the body but nobody came. It is a consequence of this poor communication and lack of humanity that ultimately – from the family's point of view – several years later they were still pursuing their grievances about Mr Williams' last hours.

The General Medical Council issued guidance in 2010 to doctors on how to deal with clinical and ethical decision making in just such a situation. (See Appendix 4) It is commonly thought that "end of life care" is applicable only when a person is dying progressively from a condition like cancer or dementia. However the GMC guidance also covers people who are at risk of suddenly dying because of a crisis:

"2. For the purposes of this guidance, patients are 'approaching the end of life' when they are likely to die within the next 12 months. This includes patients whose death is imminent (expected within a few hours or days) and those with:

- advanced, progressive, incurable conditions

- general frailty and co-existing conditions that mean they are expected to die within 12 months

- existing conditions if they are at risk of dying from a sudden acute crisis in their condition

- life-threatening acute conditions caused by sudden catastrophic events." (Appendix 4, section 2)

It is entirely understandable that in the emergency department decisions may have to be made rapidly and sometimes with patients who are unconscious or unable to communicate their wishes. In these cases, the doctors should look to family members or a person who has power of attorney.

Second, the attending doctors unilaterally came to the decision that even with admission to ICU, Mr Williams would not "recover with a reasonable quality of life". In my opinion this is an unjustified view of a subjective state (a person's quality of life) by people who are not qualified to make that judgement (see Compendium of terms). In the circumstances, this should have been discussed with the family who would be appropriate proxies to form that judgement. Again, it is partly their exclusion from the medical decision making that has led to the family suffering many years of anguish and needing to seek answers.

3. This case also raises the assertion by the family of a "fabricated and falsified" DNAR form. The hospital response, which I have seen, states that the family was allegedly consulted in this DNACPR decision. This discrepancy of recollections is a common scenario, sometimes because families were indeed involved but because of the heat of the crisis they may have forgotten; or perhaps because the doctors intended to have the discussion but for some reason this was overlooked. It is not possible for me to determine which is the case here. Yet again, taking more time to involve the family in updating them and discussing the possible outcomes of ICU admission and repeated CPR attempts, would in my opinion have reduced much of this family's distress.

4. A further concern arises in the handling of the investigation about the man's death by the police and coroner. From my understanding, the police were clearly wrong to abandon the case because the body had been cremated. There is no dispute that he had been given morphine and midazolam shortly before death and that – pharmacologically speaking – they could be directly related to his final respiratory arrest. Thus the key information for the police was already available in the medical records and could be corroborated by potential witness statements from the family and the attending doctors, and should, in my opinion, have been brought immediately to the attention of the coroner.

5. Finally, it is noteworthy that this case arose just eight months after the public announcement of the abolition of the Liverpool Care Pathway. Although the NICE guideline to replace the LCP had yet to be published two years later, it should have been clear to all clinicians from the widespread publicity after the LCP Review panel report in mid-2013, that end of life care henceforth would have to be handled with greater sensitivity, more open communication with patient and family, and an individualised and not – as in this case – a standardised blanket approach to prescribing drugs. This must apply in hospital emergency departments as in hospices and other end of life settings.

CASE STUDY 4

In 2015, Hazel aged 86 and diabetic, was admitted to the William Harvey Hospital, Ashford, Kent with pneumonia. She could talk, eat, drink and was bed/chair-bound after breaking a leg; whilst the leg had healed, it was non-weight bearing, so she needed to be hoisted.

Hazel was given an estimated discharge date and was not judged as dying. A nurse wrote that Hazel "ate a good breakfast of porridge. Swallowing normally, no issues at present. Taking all tablets orally very well." But a later instruction was that she should only have pureed food with teaspoons of fluid from nurses, although a swallow test was not performed; this instruction evolved to Nil by Mouth (NBM), although none of Hazel's family knew this. Her daily medicines were stopped, including Bisoprolol for heart failure.

Unaware of the NBM, the family fed Hazel some solid food which she wanted, the only meal she had in a week. She didn't have any swallowing problems after all.

A registrar showed prejudice towards Hazel's disability, saying, "It's not a nice life to be hoisted," before placing Hazel on End of Life.

Hazel had an IV drip, yet blood tests revealed she was dehydrated. Instead of increasing her fluid, it was decreased. Hazel was also being "treated" with a BiPAP machine: it delivered highly pressurised oxygen through a tight-fitting face mask, forcing her to breathe.

One night, Hazel had a massive drop in her blood sugar. She then lost her voice completely. No reason was given as to why she suddenly lost her voice but the consultant used it to diagnose "dying". It could have been caused by the drying effects of the BiPAP machine or by shock, as she was distressed by it.

The consultant continued to place the BiPAP on Hazel's face although she was dehydrated and no fluid was given for 24 hours. She wrote that my mother should have no nursing observations.

When I asked the consultant to put back my mother's drip, she refused, replying that Hazel had enough fluid in her body from swollen hands. She insisted my mother wouldn't become dehydrated without the drip. I asked for the oedema to be treated but this was denied.

Hazel died the day after having her drip removed, four days after her blood tests showed she was dehydrated. Her blood sugar was so low that she was not given insulin.

In spite of meetings with doctors, the family *didn't know* that:

- Hazel was NBM and her daily medicines stopped a week before she died;

- blood tests showed she was dehydrated;

- she was given less fluid when dehydrated.

Responses from authorities

In 2016, 17 apologies from my mother's consultant were given via the Chief Executive, with an admission that Mum could have eaten and drunk whatever she wanted after all.

In 2017, the Health Ombudsman partially upheld my complaint against the Trust. One failing in her care was that my mother shouldn't have been made NBM and that more feeding should have occurred. They accused the nurses of a "misunderstanding". However the records show that the consultant made the NBM decisions.

In 2020 the Serious Case Review Team from Kent Police contacted Professor Patrick Pullicino for an independent opinion on my mother's case. After studying my mother's fluid charts, Professor Pullicino's conclusion was the following:

"…that Mrs. Turner was dehydrated secondary to inadequate fluids being prescribed and/or given to her. In a person like her, with coexisting medical illness, this prolonged dehydration would certainly have contributed to her death and given that she had no fluids at all for the last 48 hours of her life, it could even have been the principal cause of death."

The response by Kent Police was that his conclusion did not constitute a crime.

I registered a complaint against Kent Police.

In 2021 I took my mother's case to the GMC, who found no malpractice by the three doctors named. I have appealed for a review of their decision.

I contacted the CQC in 2016 and 2021. They responded by saying my mother's story would be passed to the Inspector in charge of the hospital trust; also, that he might contact me, which he never has.

Medical opinion of Professor Ahmedzai

1. Hazel was an 86-year-old lady with diabetes and – from the hospital trust chief executive's letter – it appeared she also had other significant medical disorders. Her care on this admission was under the direction of a consultant geriatrician. She had a previous admission for a pleural effusion (collection of fluid in the chest outside the lung).

I have carefully read the letter from the chief executive of the hospital trust, which sheds light on medical investigations and decisions. Early in this admission she was found to have a large recurrence of this effusion, and together with a community acquired pneumonia (CAP) and a probable underlying respiratory condition (such as chronic bronchitis or chronic obstructive pulmonary disease – COPD), these put her into Type 2 respiratory failure – a serious form of lung failure. This was the reason she was placed on BiPAP (which stands for "Bi-level Positive Airways Pressure"), a form of mechanical breathing support which requires a tight-fitting face mask and can be life-saving, but is very uncomfortable for prolonged periods. The effusion was also drained of 1.5 litres of fluid.

2. It is clear that she was eating and drinking normally on admission, but according to the trust letter, she had more than one SALT assessment which later found she was in danger of aspirating (inhaling) feeds into her airways, and so was placed on a pureed diet. Eventually even that was converted to a Nil by Mouth (NBM) order. A reasonable alternative would have been to offer a nasogastric tube for prolonged liquid feeding, but according to the trust letter, she declined this intervention.

The trust also stated that the doctor responsible had later apologised for causing distress by withholding food on basis of the SALT assessment – with hindsight the doctor would have allowed the patient to eat and drink even with risk of aspiration.

3. In my opinion, a large element of this case revolves around the communication around medical decision-making on the balance of benefit and harms the patient would have experienced from different interventions – drainage of pleural effusion; relief of Type 2 respiratory failure with BiPAP; allowing the patient to eat or drink even with the risk of aspiration with serious consequences; difficulty in managing her diabetes with insulin when she was not eating; supplying adequate hydration by drip but also the risk of fluid overload; the use of potentially sedative medication such as midazolam to alleviate the distress caused by BiPAP; and the withdrawal of oral medications with sometimes no alternative ways of delivering these previously important drugs.

4. The trust admits that at one point, the team caring for Hazel recognised that she was possibly dying and changed their management accordingly. Unfortunately, the daughter's statement reveals – from the patient's and family perspective – a serious lack of discussions with them about her mother's changing condition, medical decisions being taken about her care and medications that were previously known to be important, being unilaterally stopped. NICE guideline NG31 (see Appendix 3) has a whole section of recommendations on how to manage this rapidly changing scenario, many of which focus on the importance of good communication and shared decision-making.

Thus section 1.1.1: "If it is thought that a person may be entering the last days of life, gather and document information on: ….the person's physiological, psychological, social and spiritual needs….the person's goals and wishes…the views of those important to the person about future care."

Section 1.2.1: "Establish the communication needs and expectations of people who may be entering their last days of life, taking into account: If they would like a person important to them to be present when making decisions about their care; their current level of understanding that they may be nearing death; their cognitive status and if they have any specific speech, language or other communication needs; how much information they would like to have about their prognosis; any cultural, religious, social or spiritual needs or preferences."

Section 1.2.3: "Discuss the dying person's prognosis with them (unless they do not wish to be informed) as soon as it is recognised that they may be entering the last days of life and include those important to them in the discussion if the dying person wishes."

It is clear to me from the daughter's statement, and also from the numerous apologies for deficiencies in the trust's letter, that the hospital fell short in many ways in meeting these sections of standards of the NICE guidelines. Yet the chief executive's letter concluded that "The Trust did follow the NICE guidelines for End of Life Care". In my opinion, this is disputable and many of the medical decisions taken by the doctors would be indefensible in the eyes of their peers.

5. I also detect a serious problem highlighted by this case in that the routine safeguards that should protect vulnerable older people, had failed her. These were:

a) the hospital trust admitted to many mistakes, including that she should never have been placed on the NBM order;

b) there is no evidence I could see that the trust has responded to the Ombudsman findings;

c) Kent Police initiated a serious case review and then failed to act on the findings of their own independent expert witness Professor Pullicino, and neither did they refer the case to the coroner, which in my understanding, could be seen as a serious breach of their duty to the safety of the public;

d) GMC's apparent failure to find evidence of malpractice by doctors in spite of Ombudsman findings and even though the hospital trust had admitted fundamental errors;

e) lack of action so far from CQC.

CASE STUDY 5

Background

My mother was admitted to A&E at Royal Stoke University Hospital on 7th September 2015 with one fracture (eighth rib) after a fall at home. She returned home by ambulance the next day after an assessment, with no analgesics (pain-relieving drugs) and no care plan. She was re-admitted to A&E on 10th September, following a visit from her cardiac nurse, who called out the Intermediate Care Team, who in turn called for paramedics. Her oxygen levels were low due to internal bleeding from the rib fracture. She was transferred to Ward 233 Respiratory to have a drain inserted. Her chest was scanned. The diagnosis remained the same: one fracture of the eighth rib. She was transferred to Ward 231 two weeks later.

The Hibiscrub incident

On 26th September, I was informed by a nurse from Ward 231 that my mother had swallowed some Hibiscrub in the middle of the night after asking a nurse to open it for her. She did not have dementia, so how this happened is a mystery.

My two sisters visited her that morning and they were shocked to see she was not responding, was on oxygen and seemed heavily sedated. No member of staff had spoken to my sisters.

I went up to visit her the day after and tried to get information. The male nurse looking after her was reluctant to speak when I asked questions. The consultant was treating my mother for aspiration pneumonia[1] – following Hibiscrub ingestion – as stated in clinical notes.

On 26th September, I was told that my mother was being transferred to Ward 122 for discharge, while a care package was being put in place.

Poor end of life care

On 29th September, my mother was dropped on the floor just before my sister walked onto the ward. The doctor told my sister where she was dropped. He informed my sister that this had effectively finished her.
The next day, her drip, catheter and fluids were removed. There was no drinking water by her bed, only glycerine sticks. A man arrived on the ward to give her an injection. First, he put something deep into her side. I believe

it was a syringe driver. When they rolled her over to do it, she seemed to be in excruciating pain. (We were not aware that she had other injuries at this time.) It was like seeing her being put to death.

Although the doctor told us my mother was dying, there was a moment when we were all around her bedside and she sat up on her own, smiled and reached out to hold my dad's hand. So, she was not unconscious. The staff nurse who administered the injections did this alone, which I believe was not the correct procedure. The staff nurse could not speak good English and she could not understand what we were saying.

My mother continually had breakthrough pain; I think the dosage may have been incorrect. There were moments when she was gripping the sides of the bed pleading for help. After she had passed, they did nothing to make her presentable for her family to see her. They seemed to have forgotten that we were there. We were still there one hour after my mother had died, before a nurse came back to see us.

I suspect my mother was put on the Liverpool Care Pathway even though it is now illegal, but the hospital denied this in one of their letters. They called it End of Life care.

Multiple rib fractures and haemothorax [an accumulation of blood within the pleural cavity] were found after post-mortem, which occurred after the fall. I know this because I attended the inquest, and it is stated on a letter from the coroner. A doctor informed the coroner about the fall, but the hospital trust has continually denied this happened and contradicted the coroner's letter. They are insisting my mother went in with these fractures, but she went in with only one fracture which is stated in her clinical notes.

The Trust repeated its comments to the Parliamentary and Health Service Ombudsman. My evidence appears to have been ignored. I have since contacted my MP.

Medical opinion of Professor Ahmedzai

1. This case study concerns the last month of life of an 82-year-old lady who died in hospital: the Coroner's inquest found this to be an "accidental death". Mrs Kearns had a complex medical history including serious heart valve disease, enlarged heart, irregular heart rhythm, chronic kidney disease, arthritis and previous venous thrombosis. However, until September 2015 she had been living at home.

2. Mrs Kearns was admitted to hospital as an emergency following a fall at home on 7.9.15. A chest X-ray is recorded as showing a single fractured eighth rib on the right side. She was thought by the physiotherapist to be suitable for discharge the following day. However, although rib fracture is a very painful condition, she was not discharged with pain medication (analgesia) and no care package was put in place for her recovery.

From the Parliamentary and Health Service Ombudsman (PHSO) reports and letters available to me, I can see that they found it a failure of care by the hospital trust to discharge her without a supply of analgesia and a care plan. If so, this represents an act of serious clinical negligence which would have caused the lady great distress and could have placed her at risk of further complications. Not surprisingly she was readmitted to hospital two days later, on 10.9.15, and was now found to have a sustained internal bleeding into the chest cavity on the right side (haemothorax), which required a medical procedure to drain the blood. She remained in hospital after this until her death three weeks later on 2.10.15.

3. Mrs Kearns' daughter has extensively pursued the events that befell her mother on the second admission. She became concerned about her mother's care and has diligently obtained hospital medical notes, and engaged in correspondence with the Coroner's office as well as lodging complaints with the Ombudsman. From these documents, I can see that there are three main strands to her concerns, which have partly been supported by the subsequent enquiries.

4. First, the medical diagnosis and management of the lady's rib trauma and complications have been contested. During the second admission she was found to have multiple rib fractures of the right chest. On 29.9.15 she fell in the hospital while being lifted. It is debated whether these extra rib fractures arose from this preventable fall, or whether they were actually present after her original fall at home. I believe a CT scan on 14.9.15 (i.e. before the second fall in hospital) confirmed these multiple fractures, which might not have been visible on the original simple chest X-ray, especially as the large amount of blood present could have obscured the view.

The Ombudsman thus came to the conclusion that the multiple fractures had been there from the first fall, and I am inclined to agree. However, this again raises the issue of why an elderly lady with a complex medical history should be discharged after one day, without more thorough assessments and pain medication.

5. Second, on 26.9.15, there was another preventable untoward incident in hospital regarding a bottle of the disinfectant Hibiscrub, which is ubiquitous in hospital clinical areas as a skin cleaning agent. It contains the anti-bacterial agent chlorhexidine and also a small amount of alcohol. It is not to be ingested.

An opened bottle of Hibiscrub had been placed on Mrs Kearns' bedside table and she was left unattended with it overnight. The following morning her family found her sedated and they were told that she had taken a drink of the Hibiscrub, although they were not informed of this during the night. It was thought that she now had an "aspiration pneumonia", which is inflammation or infection of the lung caused by a foreign liquid or solid being inhaled.

Correspondence between the family and the Coroner's office and Ombudsman shows that this was the cause of her final deterioration. Indeed, the death certificate which the coroner's office reissued in 2017 states "Lobar pneumonia" as the primary cause of death. ("Lobar" means only one anatomical segment of the lung is involved, which is not uncommon for a liquid aspiration.)

I have seen no evidence that she came into hospital on either admission with pneumonia – even with the multiple rib fractures and pneumothorax – and so this is most likely a hospital-acquired pneumonia, and in my opinion could be the result of another act of serious clinical negligence. Unlike the failure of care with her first hospital discharge, this breach of duty of care, in my opinion, could in fact have contributed to her death.

6. Third, the daughter has described the rapid decline in Mrs Kearns' condition after this incident, and has raised concerns about the withdrawal of her previous important medical medications and of oral fluids. In the additional documentation I saw that a Speech and Language Therapy (SALT) assessment was requested to assess swallowing ability but this was made on 1.10.15, the morning before she died. She had remained "drowsy but rousable" but the family were given only "glycerine sticks" to relieve her dry mouth. Additional documents also shown to me indicate that she had thorough medical assessments in the last days, and these concluded that she was now for "end of life care".

The daughter feels that although the Liverpool Care Pathway had been withdrawn more than a year previously, by mid-2014, in effect Mrs Kearns had died under a similar pathway. I have seen the medication chart for the final days and note that she did in fact receive what is accepted as standard end of life care medication, including analgesic and anti-vomiting drugs, and also a drug for reducing noisy breathing (sometimes called "death rattle").

However, the analgesic used was diamorphine (commonly known as heroin), and she received three small but, for her age, potentially sedating doses. Moreover from my long experience in palliative medicine, I take serious issue with the use of this drug because it is (and was then) well known that it should not be used in people like Mrs Kearns with known kidney failure because of the risk of increased side-effects. One of these is vomiting, and I suspect this is why she had received three doses of two different anti-sickness drugs.

Another consequence of using diamorphine in kidney failure is that there can be build-up of toxic by-products of this pain medicine that can cause agitation, and even paradoxically, increased pain. The daughter's description of the "excruciating" and episodic (or "breakthrough") pain that Mrs Kearns experienced in her last days could fit with this adverse effect of using morphine or diamorphine. All prescribers of the strong pain medicines called opioids are made aware of this.

On balance I am of the opinion that the withdrawal of her previous regular medication was appropriate in someone thought to be so close to death. The symptom control medication that replaced it was also justifiable – but for the choice of diamorphine for pain, which may have contributed to her having a more distressing death through vomiting and possibly increased pain and agitation. The withdrawal of intravenous fluids could be justified medically because they could have contributed to her increasing heart failure at this time, but sadly this led to her possibly being distressed by dry mouth and thirst. Dehydration, on the other hand, can aggravate anxiety, agitation and also pain, especially when morphine or diamorphine are being used.

It is well known that giving fluids through a needle placed under the skin (subcutaneous) rather than via a vein (intravenous) is safer in this situation and can provide sufficient daily fluids to keep dying people comfortable. In my opinion, it was negligent of the hospital staff not to offer Mrs Kearns subcutaneous fluids; such an act would also have allayed the anxiety of her family, who had only oral swabs to alleviate her dry mouth.

7. On balance, I agree with the Coroner's conclusion that this lady's death was "accidental", but I would go further and say that, from the evidence supplied to me, it could have been preventable and at least partly caused by negligence.

8. However, on balance, I do not think that this lady was being treated on an end of life care pathway comparable to the LCP. One of its hallmarks was the unnecessary use of syringe drivers to deliver set "cocktails" of medication. Although the daughter thought a syringe driver had been used, I did not see evidence of this in the documentation I was given. However, aspects of her end of life care medication were inappropriate and actually medically contraindicated (prohibited), and this may have led to her dying being more distressing to her and to her family present.

9. Finally, this case study has shown that the hospital trust had failed in its duty of care to her in her final illness. The Ombudsman found several aspects of her care which were deficient and was concerned that the hospital had been slow to rectify these weaknesses.

---

[1] "Aspiration pneumonia" is a form of inflammation or infection of the lung which results from foreign material (liquid or solid) being breathed (aspirated) into the windpipe and thence to the deeper lung tissues.

CASE STUDY 6

Diagnosis and poor care in hospital

My mother, Margaret, died at home in May 2016, aged 88. She had been diagnosed with cancer in February. The hospital let us take her home to die. They expected that she would die within a few days or weeks. She had been in hospital for a week with pneumonia, losing about 2kg in a week, according to records. She went into hospital clear in her mind but became confused while there. By the end of the week, we realised she hadn't been eating much and no-one in hospital had been monitoring this.

We were given morphine to administer to her at home, when she had pain. They suggested a small dose. By the time she came home, she slept all the time and was barely conscious but we fed her, first with high calorie drinks, then liquidised foods. Then she began to wake up and could eat blended food and even normal food after a while. She stopped taking morphine because she could tell us that she was not in any pain.

Misdiagnosis and incorrect treatment which could have hastened her death at home

She continued to improve for quite a while and lived a very happy three months at home, often in bed, but frequently up and about, even having the odd day out with us.

In about April, she had a knee pain and couldn't straighten it. A locum doctor came out in the night, saying the cancer had spread to her bones and gave her a larger dose of morphine with some other opiate. Now she was comatose again. A couple of days later, I spoke to a palliative care nurse at St Luke's Hospice in Kenton, who had been supporting us about her new diagnosis. He said: "They can't tell it's spread to the bones by looking at her and that's a hell of a lot of opiates to give her. It could kill her!" We took her straight off the drugs and he got her an emergency hospital appointment. They discovered it was a condition caused by fluid on the knee, drained it off in two minutes and sent her home, pain free!

Later on, one of the nurses involved in caring for my mother at home (Nurse A) warned me "Don't let them take your mum to hospital, because she will never come out".

Refusal of GP and hospice to provide fluids for the last week of her life

In May, she began deteriorating and stopped being able to swallow. She could tell me she was thirsty, so on 23rd May, I asked her GP to set up fluids for her. She refused. I then asked the hospice. They said "No". They said they didn't have the equipment to give fluids, and in any event, fluids and the relevant equipment were both expensive to provide.

I found a private doctor who came out to set up subcutaneous fluids, cheaply and easily at our home, which she remained on until her death six days later on 29th May. And after a few hours, she was able to tell me she was not thirsty and continued to indicate that, from then until her death.

First the hospice nurse, and then one of the district nurses admonished me about the fluids, explaining that they would not benefit my mother and that they could cause flooding of her system. But my mother's fluids were very well monitored and I could see that this risk was being carefully guarded against. The fluids she received were clearly proportionate and appropriate for her state of health.

Nurse A came to see me after my mother died and said she had not seen a patient die so well hydrated – without dry skin and a dry, cracked mouth - for 20 years or more, when it had been common to give fluids.

Complaint to the hospice and their response

After my mother's death, I wrote to St Luke's Hospice, Kenton, whose care team she had been under, asking why they had refused to provide fluids, and had also advised my GP not to give them. I also asked why they had misled me over the alleged difficulties of giving subcutaneous fluids, or whether their staff did not themselves understand how they worked.

They wrote back saying: "While accessing the equipment and setting up an infusion may be relatively straightforward, the monitoring required for a subcutaneous infusion at home means most community teams are unable to support this type of intervention. This intervention would require agreement by the patient's GP and District Nursing Team before they would consider starting an infusion."

However, the decision not to give fluids was a joint decision between the GP and the hospice. The GP told me she had discussed the matter with the hospice and they agreed with her that fluids should not be given.

A senior member of the hospice staff acknowledged in her letter that:

"It is possible to manage subcutaneous fluids in the patient's own home, but this is not something that the hospice nurses do." Unfortunately no-one had been willing to tell me that they were manageable at home. My mother avoided dying thirsty, and quite possibly dying of thirst, only by my good luck in finding a private doctor willing to provide fluids.

Worryingly, the hospice staff member added: "Conversations about clinically assisted hydration and nutrition are not routine i.e. we would not talk about this with every patient." I wonder how long it will be before hospice patients realise that, when they can no longer eat and drink unassisted, no help will be forthcoming. Patients must be fully informed if they are not to be assisted, even with fluids, in the days leading up to their last hours.

Medical opinion of Professor Ahmedzai

This is the case study of Margaret, an 88-year-old lady with cancer, whose last weeks were palliated – not by hospital, GP or hospice care – but by her family, who fought against ignorance and resistance to offer her what was in 2015 the standard of care recommended by national bodies like NICE and the GMC.

1. Losing 2kg in a week with a pneumonia, on a background of cancer, is not unexpected. However, for an older person who had been admitted with a "clear mind", I would have expected there to have been a nutritional assessment and a plan for her nutritional aftercare, probably including supplementary liquid feeds. Her age of 88 is immaterial – this is basic humane care and should not be modified by considerations of age. If anything, older people are more at risk of the effects of under-nutrition and specifically dehydration.

2. It is not clear to me from available information why she was being given morphine. This is given in cancer for pain or breathlessness. It is not a drug to be given just because a patient has cancer. However, especially in older people, morphine can be very sedating and this can lead to reduced ability to drink adequate fluids, as well as reduced food intake.

Medical research has been poor on measuring the adverse effects of drugs used for palliation of symptoms. Even for the most commonly used drugs in end of life care, opioid pain medications, there is very little research evidence. Thirst has hardly ever been measured in clinical trials of opioids, but the symptom of dry mouth is well recognised as a side-effect of taking opioids and so data has been collected on that. It has been shown in a high quality British systematic review of research literature (Wiffen et al, 2014),[1] that opioids in general are indeed associated with reports of dry mouth as a side effect – amounting to overall 17% of research trial subjects. However, when receiving morphine the proportion who experienced dry mouth was 47%, the highest of the 4 individual opioids studied.

The Wiffen et al study (2014) also showed that in research trials, opioids including morphine were also associated with somnolence (sedation or sleepiness) – reaching 24% in patients receiving morphine. Hence starting morphine at doses that are not justified or are not monitored runs the substantial risk of causing sleepiness, which may prevent adequate fluid and food intake; and simultaneously dry mouth, which can stimulate thirst even in the absence of biochemical dehydration.

All these factors may be moot in a person who dies within days of starting morphine, but in one who lives for many weeks and months on it, the discomfort and distress can be cumulatively serious.

3. The bedside "diagnosis" of bone spread of this lady's cancer was in my opinion, not only clinically unreasonable and unjustified, but also completely wrong. I would have expected the doctor who was responsible for this to be reported and admonished by the employer, the Royal College of GPs and the GMC.

4. The story of Margaret becoming gradually so ill that she could no longer swallow the fluids and food the family was caring enough to offer her, is a very common scenario in end of life care. It should therefore be at the forefront of the minds of all clinicians dealing in end of life, whether generalists like GPs or specialists like cancer doctors or palliative care (including hospice) staff.

NICE guideline NG31 (2015, see Appendix 3) was developed in response to the discovery of gross mismanagement of some end of life care delivered under the LCP. One of the commonest reasons for complaint from bereaved carers and the public was the reluctance of clinicians to offer fluids to dying people, especially if they were placed "on the pathway".

NG31 robustly addressed this issue and recommended considering the possibility of administering clinically assisted hydration (by tube or drip) to patients no longer able to swallow. By May 2016 this should have been common knowledge amongst all doctors and nurses giving healthcare and palliative care in particular.

The GMC (2010) has also delivered clear guidance to doctors about how to assess people for hydration and their duties to offer assistance:

"If a patient is in the end stage of a disease or condition, but you judge that their death is not expected within hours or days, you must provide clinically assisted nutrition or hydration if it would be of overall benefit to them, taking into account the patient's beliefs and values, any previous request for nutrition or hydration by tube or drip and any other views they previously expressed about their care. The patient's request must be given weight and, when the benefits, burdens and risks are finely balanced, will usually be the deciding factor." (see Appendix 4)

Thus I find it to be, from the evidence I have seen, a breach of duty of care by the clinicians cited in this case study who denied the lady the comfort and dignity of having assisted fluids. The reasons they gave including expense, lack of training and equipment are absolutely immaterial, because offering assisted hydration in different ways has been standard practice in hospitals, and indeed in many hospices, for decades and the knowledge and equipment are readily available. In my experience and opinion, denying this patient a trial of assisted hydration would not have been supported by a group of medical peers at this point in time.

I read the letter from the Director of Nursing and Patient Services at St Luke's Hospice in response to the family's questions about why they did not offer Margaret assisted fluids. I find their justifications unconvincing. It is clear that this hospice was not – 18 months after the publication of the NICE guideline NG31 – prepared to accept and implement its recommendations. This is lamentable and worthy of a complaint to the Care Quality Commission.

5. It was fortunate for the family in this case to have found a private doctor who was prepared and skilled to perform subcutaneous hydration in the lady's home. The observation from one of the nurses caring for her, that she had not seen such a well-hydrated dying person in 20 years, adds to the indictment against those who had denied the fluids. Had it not been for Margaret's family persisting and not accepting the refusals, coupled with their ability to giving loving care to their mother in her home, I am in no doubt that she would have died many days or weeks before her "natural" end of life, and in a greater level of distress.

6. In conclusion, in my opinion this lady's end of life care fell far short of the standards recommended in NICE guideline NG31, the GMC guidance on assisted hydration at end of life – and of the general duty of care by all healthcare practitioners, nurses included. From the evidence I have seen, this could be a negligent breach of their duty of care, contributing to her discomfort and distress and, had it not been for her family's care and persistence, likely to have led to an earlier death.

---

[1] Wiffen PJ, Derry S, Moore RA. Impact of morphine, fentanyl, oxycodone or codeine on patient consciousness, appetite and thirst when used to treat cancer pain. Cochrane Database of Systematic Reviews 2014, Issue 5. Art. No.: CD011056. DOI: 10.1002/14651858.CD011056.pub2.

CASE STUDY 7

Our concerns

Our daughter Laura Jane Booth received excellent care at the Sheffield Children's Hospital for her first 18 years. Laura had learning disabilities and complex medical conditions from birth (partial trisomy 13, also called Patau's syndrome; diabetes; Crohn's disease; juvenile arthritis). In spite of these conditions, she was communicative, and so kind and caring and loved life. She could not speak but understood simple questions and communicated by limited sign language. We were devoted to Laura and love and miss her so much. Life will never be the same without her.

At 21, Laura went into Sheffield's Royal Hallamshire Hospital for a routine corneal eye operation in September 2016 but could not have the operation because she had been left for two weeks with very low potassium. This was due to a failing by the blood lab and the pre-op assessment department.

The subsequent care Laura received at the hospital on this admission was appalling. She had no nutrition for the entire three and a half weeks she was in. The senior doctors would not make any decision about her feeding – they came up with more reasons about the risks of 'refeeding syndrome' than about benefits of feeding her, so Laura died of malnutrition. She was denied her human rights and in spite of being known to have reduced mental capacity, they failed to follow the Mental Capacity Act. Although she was starved of food, she became fluid-overloaded, with water coming out all over her body. She could not move her own legs. They were too heavy, so we had to keep moving them for her.

Laura even went to intensive care but was only there three days and while there, still nobody did anything about Laura not feeding. She was then sent back to the ward where a lot of senior doctors and even some professors could not agree a plan. They spent the entire three and a half weeks doing nothing but passing the buck between themselves. We constantly told them about our concerns every day but it became clear that no-one would listen to anything we said. They did not even pay attention by looking at Laura or trying to communicate with her.

At the time of Laura's death, we believed she was still considered to be in hospital for routine surgery. Nobody ever told us that she was on an end of life care pathway. But after she died and at the Inquest they tried to say that Laura had outlived her time with multiple conditions.

Documentary evidence

We were finally granted an inquest which took place four and a half years after her death. There was a Coroner's statement and we eventually had two death certificates - the first one issued by the Trust in 2016, and the second one by the Coroner in 2021.

Among the Coroner's findings are (*verbatim*):

"a. Laura's nutritional intake was not given sufficient weight or discussion from 29 September 2016 to the 19 October 2016.

b. Clinical decisions were made for Laura unlawfully.

c. Laura should have been discussed in a multidisciplinary team and a formal plan and strategy should have been developed by no later than 7 October 2016 for nutrition.

d. Alternative feeding, whether via nasogastric tube or total parenteral nutrition should have been tried and commenced between 29 September 2016 and no later than 14 October 2016.

e. The decision not to adequately manage Laura's nutrition was a gross failure of her care.

f. Laura's malnutrition contributed to her death and contributed in a way which was more than minimal, negligible or trivial."

Specific action/s that led to her death

We believe that the doctors' not having a plan of care for Laura and their inability to provide even basic care for Laura, meant she died of malnutrition, neglect, and in breach of her human rights.

This is confirmed by the Coroner's conclusion and in the revised death certificate she issued, which states: "She became unwell whilst she was a patient at the hospital and amongst other illnesses she also developed malnutrition due to inadequate management of her nutritional needs. Her death was contributed to by neglect."

Complaints to the hospital

We attended a meeting with the Trust in 2017. They told us they did not have funding for Laura's care, and the adult hospital is not set up for people like Laura with complex medical conditions.

Is there a legal case ongoing?

The legal case concluded in 2021 with the Coroner's inquest. It took us four and a half years to get an inquest after the doctors had put her death as "natural causes".

Complaints to the authorities

We have lodged complaints with the hospital trust, Sheffield Clinical Commissioning Group, and NHS England. The NHS did an independent report that went on for 12 months. We spoke with the CQC which did a full inspection of Sheffield Teaching Hospitals Trust in 2021, in which they found very poor services and told them to improve them. Even in November 2021 CQC found 'some improvement, but not enough'. We are waiting for their next follow-up inspection.

Medical opinion of Professor Ahmedzai

Declaration of interest: I was one of the clinicians who had previously been involved in the care of the young lady, but I retired from practice a year before her final admission. I had befriended her parents and was invited by the Coroner to give informal evidence in support of their position at the inquest.

There are four important lessons that this very sad case teaches.

1. It is shocking that a 21-year-old lady with learning disabilities and multiple medical conditions (which were all under control) went into hospital for a 'routine' eye operation, and died three and a half weeks later without her nutritional needs being met, such that a Coroner found that malnutrition contributed significantly to her death. This was despite her parents asking daily for assessments and clinical assistance with nutrition to be given. The case highlighted the hospital trust's lack of joined-up care, with each specialist looking to another to make the decision to start feeding. As the parents pointed out, the only arguments given were about the potential dangers of feeding, not the very real one of not feeding.

2. Sadly this case reflects what we have known for many years from the LeDeR reports (Learning Disability Mortality Review Programme) that people with learning disabilities have a much higher rate of complications if they are admitted to hospital and a much higher death rate for the same conditions, compared to non-disabled people.(LeDeR, 2021) The risk here was compounded because the young lady had recently been "transitioned" from the children's hospital to the adult hospital, which later admitted it had made insufficient preparations to take on her case. This is a scandalous situation and I am aware the Coroner herself has taken steps to escalate the lessons of this case to a national level in her profession to help prevent future deaths.

3. The observation that the hospital never called a "Best Interests" meeting for this person who was clearly incapable of making medical decisions, was in the Coroner's words "unlawful". This is in clear breach of the Mental Capacity Act (2005). One year after the inquest we are unaware of any staff having been censured or suspended. In the light of the preceding Gosport and Stafford hospital scandals, this is unforgivable.

4. This case also shows us that the family's persevering with Laura's case after they were unhappy with the medical team's management during life and their dismissal of concerns after her death, resulted in a dramatic reappraisal and reversal of the conclusion. The initial death certificate stated the cause of death as being:

"1 (a) Pulmonary oedema, Respiratory Failure due to Hypolabuminaemia and Pneumonia

(b) Crohn's disease, Hypogammaglobulinaemia, Arthritis (Treated)

(c) Partial Trisomy Thirteen"

After her inquest, the Coroner issued a new death certificate which gave the cause of death as:

"1 (a) Respiratory Failure

(b) Bronchopneumonia

(c) Partial Trisomy 13 (Patau's syndrome)

II Malnutrition, Immunodeficiency (treated), Crohn's disease (treated), Insulin-dependent Diabetes Mellitus, Juvenile Arthritis (treated)."

It is clear to me that the hospital trust's first death certification was erroneous because it did not acknowledge the plain fact that the patient had not been fed for three and half weeks. The Coroner's certificate has addressed that error and laid clear blame on the hospital and its staff for causing this failure:

"...she also developed malnutrition due to inadequate management of her nutritional needs. Her death was contributed to by neglect."

Sadly, in most cases bereaved relatives are insufficiently informed of their rights or supported in the practicalities to seek further explanations, let alone press for years for an inquest.

5. Finally, it should have been plain to any clinical observer – or indeed a layperson - that a person who was not eating or drinking for three and a half weeks and who suffered hospital-acquired infections was at risk of dying. That this was never conveyed to the parents is another breach of duty of care and goes against the recommendations of NICE guideline NG31 (see Appendix 3) about the recognition of the possibility of dying, and the need to discuss this with the patient (if competent), or with the family.

CASE STUDY 8

Overview

I am Christine Pulfrey and my mum sadly died in February 2017 in Hull Royal Infirmary. I understand that she died due to not being given food and hydration.

Mum was 86 years old and very fit. She went into Spire Hospital in Hull for a routine knee operation. She was given a general anaesthetic instead of a spinal block. She had had a spinal block before and was expecting the same. My mum was very deaf but I was not allowed to sit in with her during the discussion with the anaesthetist, which would have helped.

Mum developed a post-operative pneumonia with concurrent heart failure after the operation and due to Spire being a private hospital (although Mum was an NHS patient) they did not have the facilities to deal with her. She was fed very little and the care left a lot to be desired.

Hospital transfer

She was transferred to Hull Royal Infirmary for supposedly better treatment. My husband and I accompanied her there. We were advised that she would receive antibiotic injections, blood samples would be taken to identify the infection, she would be given a drip to hydrate her and physio to help her with her breathing. Before we left, they attached a cannula and gave her the antibiotic injection and attached a drip. She seemed settled when we left.

Further developments

When I arrived the next day she had on an oxygen mask and a drip, and her demeanour was reasonable. She indicated that she was very thirsty and wanted a drink, but was refused with the explanation that the water might go into her lungs and not her stomach. Her drip had run out when I was leaving at 8 o'clock, so I advised the nurse. When I rang later at 10 o'clock, she advised me the drip had not been replaced.

When I lost my temper with the staff, they attached a drip and cannula and gave her a further antibiotic injection. She improved vastly with hydration and antibiotics. She was very hungry but was refused food and was told she would be fed through her nose. She was also advised that she could not be fed until her throat had been checked and a dietician had prescribed her the feed.

We were telephoned in the early hours and advised she had deteriorated and needed to be on a ventilator. When we arrived at the ICU, we were advised that she was too ill and that it would be too traumatic to put her on a ventilator. We took their advice, but after being given an injection, she came round.

When she went back to the ward they decided to try to drain her lungs and this was dealt with by someone who had no idea what he was doing. I witnessed it because I was sitting outside the curtain. A couple of days before she died she was fitted with the nasal tube, but she was never fed at all during her time at the hospital. She eventually deteriorated and we were advised to let her pass away with the help of drugs.

Deprived of hydration and food

When I was with Mum and she received hydration, she improved. However, from the day she went into Hull Royal on 2nd February – when she was only given a glass of water – she was not fed anything after this until the day she died, which was seven days later. In her lucid moments, Mum said she was hungry and wanted something to eat and drink, but this was not permitted. The answer was that it might go into her lungs. I was only allowed to be there at visiting times and I felt that things went wrong when I was not allowed to be there and supervise her care. The hydration was removed, the antibiotic injections were not given and she was never fed.

I do believe my mum was deliberately deprived of hydration and food and was neglected because she was 86 years old. She was not frail and was in good form when she went into hospital. I do believe she might have been able to fight the infection had she been given the right treatment and not been deprived of food and water. I still feel guilty to this day that I did not intervene more than I did. She was very vulnerable as she was deaf. They lost her hearing aids, so she would have had no idea what was going on. When she died she looked as if she had been starved, like the people who were starved in the concentration camps. The memories of it all are still with me to this day. I felt I had not protected my mum when she needed me most. I hope by my story being published, other people will not have to go through what we did as a family.

Medical opinion of Professor Ahmedzai

1. This case arose just over a year after NICE guideline NG31 was published (see Appendix 3). For any NHS place of care (and arguably also any private institution) to defy its recommendations about the need for recognising dying and the reciprocal possibility of improvement, and then taking appropriate actions, could be seen as a breach of duty of care, unless the medical team could prove that the guideline did not apply to this specific case.

Similarly, the subsequent failure to respect the patient's and family's wishes also, in my opinion, breached her human rights and caused her family unnecessary mental distress. A further negligent breach of her rights and dignity arose when they lost her hearing aid, which left her unable to communicate.

2. GMC guidance (2010, see Appendix 4) discusses the clinical and ethical arguments about giving assisted nutrition and hydration to adults in hospital.

First, for adults who have mental capacity, it states:

"If you assess that clinically assisted nutrition or hydration would not be clinically appropriate, you must monitor the patient's condition and reassess the benefits, burdens and risks of providing clinically assisted nutrition or hydration as the patient's condition changes. If a patient asks you to provide nutrition or hydration by tube or drip, you should discuss the issues with the patient and explore the reasons for their request. You must reassess the benefits, burdens and risks of providing the treatment requested, giving weight to the patient's wishes and values. When the benefits, burdens and risks are finely balanced, the patient's request will usually be the deciding factor."

For patients who lack capacity for medical decision-making but are not expected to die in hours or days, GMC guidance states:

"If a patient is in the end stage of a disease or condition, but you judge that their death is not expected within hours or days, you must provide clinically assisted nutrition or hydration if it would be of overall benefit to them, taking into account the patient's beliefs and values, any previous request for nutrition or hydration by tube or drip and any other views they previously expressed about their care. The patient's request must be given weight and,

WHEN 'END OF LIFE CARE' GOES WRONG

when the benefits, burdens and risks are finely balanced, will usually be the deciding factor."

3. The specific aspect of withholding (and indeed, actually withdrawing) clinically assisted hydration for a previously fit older person who came into hospital for an elective procedure, represents to me (and I believe, to a majority of medical practitioners) an act of negligence which could have contributed to her discomfort and to death.

4. NICE guideline NG31 clearly states (Recommendation 14.1):
"Support the dying person to drink if they wish to and are able to. Check for any difficulties, such as swallowing problems or risk of aspiration. Discuss the risks and benefits of continuing to drink, with the dying person, and those involved in the dying person's care."

It seems to me that there might have been at least one attempt to feed her, which may have led to an aspiration (that is, the feed going down the "wrong way" into her windpipe) – and this led the ward team to unilaterally make the decision not to offer her any more by mouth. It is not clear to me whether this was supported by a Speech and Language Therapy (SALT) assessment; why they took so long to pass a nasogastric tube for feeding/ fluids; and why in fact feeding was not given when one was finally passed. These should have been routine practice in the ICU and I am at a loss to understand why assisted hydration was not offered, particularly while she was in that setting.

5. The family's view that she could have fought the infection and recovered with adequate feeding and fluids is a contestable point – this is discussed in NG31 which found that the research evidence is inconclusive on these outcomes. However, the guideline clearly states that patients can be given the benefit of the doubt, and there is also no overwhelming evidence that offering fluids could have harmed her.

For humane reasons, in my opinion she should have had the benefit of a trial of assisted hydration – either by a tube placed through the nose or through a drip – at the earliest opportunity after the family requested it.

6. A final point in considering this case is how the daughter was made to feel "guilty that she did not intervene" more than she did in her mother's care; and she "felt I had not protected my mum when she needed me most". In fact I believe the daughter had clearly gone further than many, less articulate, relatives might have done in similar circumstances. One worries how much long-lasting mental distress is caused by such badly managed end of life care situations.

WHEN 'END OF LIFE CARE' GOES WRONG

CASE STUDY 9

Velindre Cancer Hospital, Cardiff

Mark, my husband, had been diagnosed with terminal lung cancer which had spread to his brain. On 7th October 2017, he had gone to hospital as an outpatient for a blood transfusion and had been admitted with a chest infection. After a few days, there were signs of improvement and plans were being made for him to go home. The hospital arranged our wedding at this time and they were happy for him to stay a few more days, until after the ceremony.

We married on 15th October. This was the first time since admittance that Mark needed to be hoisted into a wheelchair for the ceremony. Two days later, the palliative care doctor asked whether Mark wanted to continue the treatment for pneumonia at Velindre or Marie Curie.

Marie Curie Hospice, Cardiff

On 18th October, Mark was transferred to the hospice. He had severe stomach pains at 3pm and a doctor finally arrived at 6pm. When asked if Mark should be given suppositories, he argued but reluctantly gave in. Mark hadn't opened his bowels for four days. A nurse and a healthcare assistant arrived, and each grabbed a side of my husband's pants, whipping them down, followed by the nurse commenting, "You have a cute bum!"

Mark vomited faecal matter filling two bowls before he could pass any stools, then filled two bedpans. I was told faecal vomiting was a usual occurrence. While Mark was using the bedpan, a nurse entered, saying there was a call for him. I mentioned that Mark hadn't been drinking enough and queried a rash on his left side, as he yelped while being moved. My observations were ignored. Mark declined food while he was sitting on a bedpan. He didn't receive any food prior to me leaving at 7.30pm. He appeared relaxed with no problems.

On 19th October, Mark appeared dazed and was hallucinating and unusually sleepy. I told the consultant that I thought Mark was dehydrated, but she said dismissively: "It could be signs that the body is shutting down". She also said that if I still felt the same tomorrow, they could try giving him some fluids then, but not intravenously, as this could be potentially dangerous for him. I disagreed with her decisions but she was adamant that this was the only option. Mark barely spoke the entire day and didn't move at all. He hadn't been drinking or eating due to sleeping most of the day. No food was delivered prior to me leaving at 7pm. He was settled with bedrails in position.

On 20th October, the ward sister informed me that Mark had fallen out of bed. She didn't know why the bedrails weren't in position. I spoke to the hospice manager, as the care was getting worse day by day, informing her about the following concerns: waiting hours for a doctor; my ongoing concerns with Mark's hydration status; lack of food; poor quality of nursing; the overall lack of dignity shown; Mark's fall; and his request to be moved out of the hospice as soon as possible. She laughed at the nurse's comment about Mark's cute posterior, stating that her staff liked to have banter with the patients! She refused to make any arrangements to move him out of the hospice, as it was a Friday morning, explaining that we would have to wait another three days until after the weekend. A couple of hours after our meeting, Mark was moved to the superior death room with a sea view near the nursing station, where the consultant and GP attended briefly together. I asked the consultant to look at the rash that had been ignored by nursing staff. She immediately diagnosed shingles.

After further requests, the subcutaneous fluids were finally initiated halfway through the day. Mark told me he was left lying on the floor for ages before anyone came, also stating "They are killing me in here!" Other than this brief conversation in the morning, he just lay there staring and didn't move for the duration of the day. I fed and gave him fluids orally. I stayed the night in his room.

On 21st October, Mark hadn't moved or spoken. The same one-litre bag of subcutaneous fluids was still being given from the previous day. After making numerous complaints, it was discovered that the drip wasn't working, the bag being eventually discarded and changed for a new one, halfway through the day. Up to this point, Mark hadn't even been given half a litre of fluids in 24 hours!

On the next day, the second one-litre fluid bag was still being given from the previous day. Mark stared the entire day, not moving. He was very hungry when I fed him. Around 10pm, the head nurse gave him a dose of Oramorph, as he was slightly short of breath. An hour or so later, his breathing became noisy, so she gave him a dose of hyoscine hydrobromide, after which he became peaceful. She brought in a healthcare assistant. They repositioned him from his side to his back, as his breathing became laboured. We were then told Mark was dying. He died in the early hours of 23rd October. He was 52. Throughout his admission, I was not aware of any moral support being given to Mark, and none was given to me.

Complaints

We have complained in writing to the Velindre Hospital, who decided on the death path; Marie Care Hospice, who executed it; and the Heath Inspectorate Wales, who were not interested. We made verbal complaints to the medical practitioners. I also complained to the Ombudsman in Wales but was informed that I was out of time. The whole process was so mentally exhausting.

Medical opinion of Professor Ahmedzai

1. This case story focuses on the last four days in the life of a man with lung cancer that had spread to his brain, abdomen and other areas of his body, in spite of standard oncological care consisting of high dose palliative radiotherapy, followed by palliative chemotherapy and further radiotherapy to the brain. At this point he was thought to have progressive disease and transfer was arranged to the local Marie Curie hospice. As a sign of good end of life care, the hospital actually arranged for the patient, Mark, to be married in the hospital before his transfer.

2. After transfer, Mark's wife had raised a large number of complaints regarding his care in the hospice. The main concern I have in this case is the response of the hospice to the wife's quite reasonable request for Mark to receive assisted hydration. He appeared sleepy and was hallucinating, which could indeed be features of dehydration. The hospice medical staff did not apparently do blood tests to check his hydration status and kidney function. They appeared to disagree with his wife about the need and the mode of hydration.

Given what we know about the shortcomings of end of life care in some settings, especially during the period when the LCP was in active use, it is worrying to me that the hospice was so dismissive of the request for assisted hydration. The doctors should have been aware of the GMC guidance from 2010 which made it clear that requests for hydration from patients and families at the end of life should be considered seriously, and in the GMC's words (see Appendix 4):

Section 124:

"If a patient has previously requested that nutrition or hydration be provided until their death, or those close to the patient are sure that this is what the patient wanted, the patient's wishes must be given weight and, when the benefits, burdens and risks are finely balanced, will usually be the deciding factor."

NICE guideline NG31 (2015, see Appendix 3) also clearly states the duties of staff to consider a trial of assisted hydration if the patient is unable to take oral fluids adequately.

In the event, subcutaneous fluids were indeed started. However, from the wife's account it appears that this was "hit and miss" and from the records I have seen, I doubt whether Mark actually received sufficient fluids in the time the infusion was running before he died.

In my 30 years' experience of end of life care, it is common to find non-specialist settings where staff may not be familiar with the siting and monitoring of subcutaneous infusions. However, I am shocked to read that in a British hospice in 2017, the staff first prevaricated about placing the subcutaneous cannula and then did not perform this correctly. In my opinion this would appear to be a negligent breach of duty of care, with respect to both GMC (2010) and NICE (NG31, 2015) guidelines.

3. In answer to the wife's complaints about the management of hydration, the hospital trust's response (with contributions from the hospice medical director and other staff) found that for this topic there was no cause for complaint. Indeed, the trust found: "The investigation has not identified any problems relating to the direct provision of MC's clinical care and treatment or the level of information, support and advice he received from the clinical teams." Oddly enough though, it also stated "All clinicians involved in the care and treatment of MC have reflected on the concerns raised and will use the feedback as an opportunity to inform their practice". This sounds to me very much like a "boiler-plate text", ie a standard cut and pasted reply, and not sincere. In my experience of conducting dozens of medicolegal case reviews, I have rarely found one which is so dismissive of <u>all</u> of the plaintiff's claims.

4. Many of the wife's complaints refer to aspects of the indignities that Mark was exposed to in his short stay at the hospice. The hospital notes show that Mark had a history of constipation, but the cause was not evident. It is likely that opioid medication (usually morphine) for pain and breathlessness had played a part, but I am aware that he had abdominal spread from his cancer and therefore malignant bowel obstruction may have played a role.

After suppositories (laxative medication tablets inserted into rectum) were given, he had an intense response – filling two bedpans – and had "faecal vomiting". In my experience the reporting of "faecal vomiting" is not, as the hospice staff declared, a "usual" accompaniment to simple constipation. It will have been very distressing for the patient and his wife to experience. In my opinion, to call this a usual feature would have been inconsiderate and denied the patient his dignity.

Mark's wife recalls this incident because she also describes two nursing staff brusquely taking down his pants and making a flippant remark about his bottom, which seems to me inappropriate at the least, and probably a breach of his right to dignity. But when she had mentioned this to the hospice manager, it was put down as "banter". I was also saddened that the trust's letter of response to the wife's complaints appears to disregard this incident.

5. By the wife's account (and additional documentation I have seen), when Mark was initially transferred, he had been capable of eating but no food was available in the hospice in the evening because the kitchen was shut. Having worked in the hospice sector full-time clinically for nine years and then intermittently for a further 21 years, visiting patients in hospices as part of my clinical duties, I cannot recall a single hospice which would not have made efforts to supply a hungry patient with food at any time of day or night. I therefore find the alleged refusal of the hospice to supply Mark with food inexplicable and falling well below the standard of British hospice care.

6. Extensive documentation supplied by Mark's wife showed she raised other concerns regarding the way that Mark's DNACPR form was handled in the hospice: again this was dismissed by the enquiry. She also asked whether he had been placed on the LCP or a variation of it: again this was rejected. However, my conclusion is that the hospice in question was operating in a way that could have been representative of those who were misusing the LCP prior to the Neuberger Review panel's verdict to stop it.

Moreover, in my opinion the hospice medical and nursing teams could be regarded as being in breach of their duties to the patient generally with respect to human dignity; and specifically, that they could have acted negligently with regard to the clear guidance from NICE and the GMC on ensuring hydration.

CASE STUDY 10

Below are separate stories of a hospice nurse's father and mother.

Case 1: testimony about my father

Background

My father was a 92-year-old gentleman who was in reasonably good health but was disabled, having lost the use of his legs due to a spine problem. He occasionally suffered from urine infections and chest infections. He was wheelchair-bound but his cognition was excellent and he enjoyed life. He had carers four times a day to assist him to get into his electric wheelchair, which he was well able to operate himself.

Diagnosis

In November 2017, my father was admitted to hospital after being found unconscious at home. An ambulance was called. After tests in the hospital, the doctor told me this was "a terminal event", and that my father was suffering from septicaemia and multiple organ failure. He wanted to change my father's resuscitation status to "Do Not Resuscitate". I expressed my worries that I didn't want my dad to starve or dehydrate to death. I was also worried that if I signed the DNR, it could lead to him not being fed. The doctor responded in quite an aggressive manner to my not wanting him to starve or dehydrate to death, saying that he would not give him "futile treatment".

I was perplexed that food and drink was regarded as a treatment. He brutishly told me not to believe what I might have read in the *Daily Mail*. My experiences, however, were not taken from what I read in a newspaper but were based on my experiences as a paediatric hospice nurse, where I first encountered fluids being withdrawn in palliative care.

My experiences had taught me that if fluids are withdrawn there can be no way back if things turn around. I appealed to the doctor, to persuade him at the very least to keep his intravenous fluids and antibiotics continuing. The doctor did eventually agree. The following morning my dad woke up and ate a whole bowl of porridge and drank a cup of tea. He went home a few weeks later. If I had not intervened, I believe my father would not have survived this.

Outcome

My father spent some lovely time at home with his family after this hospital stay. My concerns, however, were how a misdiagnosis of a terminal event could result in somebody not being fed or hydrated, which would lead to certain death. To consider food and fluids as a futile treatment is most worrying, even if it is a terminal event.

Case 2: testimony about my mother

Resuscitation issue and its consequences and concerns (2019)

My mother, who was 88 years old and who had Alzheimer's, was admitted to hospital with a fairly minor chest infection. I was approached by the doctor who was keen to establish her resuscitation status. My mother was asked whether she wanted to be resuscitated. She immediately told the doctor to ask me, as I would know what to do. My mother trusted me with this. I voiced my concern that end of life was not yet in sight and I felt uncomfortable about signing "no" to resuscitation.

My mother was then told that cardiopulmonary resuscitation would break her ribs, which frightened her. I explained that I had worked in a children's hospice and on many occasions witnessed that when parents signed a "no" for resuscitation, situations would follow where the "no" status was misconstrued as meaning "no" to life-sustaining treatments such as intravenous antibiotics/intravenous fluids.

A more senior doctor was called, who said that she would override my decision even though I had Power of Attorney (POA) for my mother. After leaving the hospital a few weeks later, I received documentation indicating that Mum had a "no" assigned to her resuscitation status. I immediately wrote to the hospital and complained, stating what had happened and my concerns that it would prevent her from having life-sustaining treatments. I had received a letter back from the doctor explaining that they had spoken to my mother without me being present, and had gained consent not to resuscitate her (even though she had dementia and I had a POA).

I had received another letter further to my complaint from the doctor in charge of my mother, assuring me that it would not affect her receiving life-sustaining treatments and fluids if she needed them.

Concerns regarding consequences of resuscitation status further down the line (April 2020)

My mother was in hospital recovering from a broken hip. She caught COVID-19 in hospital and fought and beat it. She recovered from this threat only to face a greater threat. The hospital doctor called me to say that Mum was ready for discharge and that we might want to consider not giving her fluids and/or antibiotics, if she became ill again.

My previous concerns about the "no" to resuscitation were now being confirmed. I challenged this by saying that the Liverpool Care Pathway had been outlawed and banned for not including fluids in palliative care (my mum was not even at the end of her life yet and had just won her battle against COVID). The doctor didn't pursue the questioning further and the situation was averted. Mum came home and spent a good year at home, drinking plenty of fluids herself with help from us and her live-in carer.

Concerns about no fluids

Mum was in hospital in July 2021. There was a phone call from the doctor, saying that I needed to come to the hospital as she was at "end of life" now. It was said that her blood results were suggesting this. He said that she was not drinking, so it would be quick (a few days). I asked whether she could have comfort subcutaneous fluids since she was not drinking. Again I mentioned the Liverpool Care Pathway being outlawed for not including fluids. He said he would speak to the consultant, who must have said no, as no fluids were up when I arrived.

As my mother was thought to be at the "end of life", they allowed me to visit whenever I wanted. My mother was thirsty and she was drinking. The new threat now was, would she be given drinks when I was not in the hospital?

I visited on one of the days and found her hanging out of the bed. When I asked her what she was doing, she said she was trying to get a drink. I felt it difficult to leave her as I had no confidence that fluids would be given. I stayed every day for the next two weeks and she began to thrive again – only because I was giving her fluids. If I had not intervened, I felt sure she would have dehydrated to death. She was eventually discharged to a nursing home where she remained for a few weeks before we lost her. They did give her oral fluids in the nursing home but could not offer subcutaneous fluids if her swallow deteriorated, as they were not trained in this.

I have not written to my MP about the above as I had already written extensively to Peter Luff (MP) about palliative care issues such as the above when I worked as a nurse in a children's hospice. I also wrote about this to the BMA.

Medical opinion of Professor Ahmedzai

The following two case studies are remarkable in that they are of a couple, father and mother to the person who submitted them. Moreover, she had been a paediatric hospice nurse and had direct experience that accepting a DNACPR decision could lead to the withdrawal of fluids in dying patients.

Case 1 – Father

1. The first case is of the 92-year-old father, who was mentally fit and enjoying life with his electric wheelchair, but was admitted to hospital with an acute medical event. We are told that he had multiple organ failure from septicaemia – a serious situation from which, to be fair, many nonagenarians would not survive. But thanks to his daughter's nursing experience and her persistence, he was able to overcome this situation and return home.

2. We are told that the patient was unconscious and after being told by the attending doctor that he was in a "terminal event", the daughter was apparently asked to change an existing CPR decision from Yes to No. It is noteworthy that although the daughter may have accepted that her father might be terminally ill, from her practical experience she felt that agreeing to a "Do not attempt cardiopulmonary resuscitation" (DNACPR) decision could lead to her father having a hastened and more distressing death because of staff withholding fluids and possibly antibiotics. It appears as if the doctor was aggressive and intimidating. I suspect this is a very common scenario, and sadly one in which many less knowledgeable or self-confident relatives will acquiesce to DNACPR.

3. What I found most worrying here was the doctor's argument that fluids would be "futile treatment". Technically, giving clinically assisted hydration to an unconscious patient is indeed regarded as a medical treatment.

However, the General Medical Council (GMC) has made it clear that the duty of doctors is to listen to the views of people near the end of life and to their families:

"114. Nutrition and hydration provided by tube or drip are regarded in law as medical treatment, and should be treated in the same way as other medical interventions. Nonetheless, some people see nutrition and hydration, whether taken orally or by tube or drip, as part of basic nurture for the patient that should almost always be provided. For this reason it is especially important that you listen to and consider the views of the patient and of those close to them (including their cultural and religious views) and explain the issues to be considered, including the benefits, burdens and risks of providing clinically assisted nutrition and hydration." (GMC, 2010, see Appendix 4).

Further, the GMC guidance to doctors states:

"124. If a patient has previously requested that nutrition or hydration be provided until their death, or those close to the patient are sure that this is what the patient wanted, the patient's wishes must be given weight and, when the benefits, burdens and risks are finely balanced, will usually be the deciding factor."

Case 2 – Mother

1. In this second case study from the same daughter, four years after her father's death she was faced with a similar situation concerning her mother, aged 88 years. Once again she was asked to agree to DNACPR but knew that accepting this could often – quite wrongly – be interpreted by hospital staff as condoning withdrawal of other forms of life-sustaining and even comfort treatments, such as giving assistance with drinking or receiving of fluids.

However, I have seen a letter from the hospital which shows that the mother was assessed later for mental capacity to make the decision herself and had herself agreed to DNACPR and so her decision, on the basis of this hospital documentation, cannot be disputed. Nevertheless, subsequent events concerning hydration proved the daughter correct in her concerns about other treatment decisions.

2. This case is a very good example of a "blanket" approach potentially being applied to older people regarding CPR status. It was clear that this elderly lady with Alzheimer's had intercurrent problems requiring hospital admission and she was capable – up to that point - of making good recoveries. However, the implication is that if any of these intercurrent conditions led to a cardiac event such as a slowed or irregular heartbeat, the chances are that she would not have survived.

3. I am bound to add that – in principle – it could also be argued that raising the issue of CPR well in advance of end of life is helpful for some patients and families in preparation for "advance care planning". Many have never considered how they would react to a DNACPR decision request and – if introduced tactfully and respectfully – it may lead to better end of life care plans.

4. In this situation, the daughter was knowledgeable and knew from experience that accepting a DNACPR decision could lead to withdrawal of other forms of end of life care. She was proved right in her concerns, when her mother became very ill after being unable to drink. We are told that the lady was treated quite inappropriately by being given no opportunity for assistance with drinking (as she was indeed capable with help) or of assisted hydration with a drip. This is probably a very common scenario and indeed one which was raised many times with the Neuberger LCP Review Panel that eventually recommended banning the LCP (see Appendix 1).

5. A further issue this case raises is that the nursing home to which she was sent, was untrained and unequipped to offer clinically assisted hydration. This is quite unacceptable in the light of NICE guideline NG31 (2015), which recommended clearly:

"1.4.8 Consider a therapeutic trial of clinically assisted hydration if the person has distressing symptoms or signs that could be associated with dehydration, such as thirst or delirium, and oral hydration is inadequate." (see Appendix 3)

As the population inexorably ages, more people are likely to end their days in care or nursing homes. In my opinion, it should be a priority for medical and nursing bodies to ensure that these settings are equipped and trained in the use of assisted forms of hydration for appropriate cases, at the end of life.

CASE STUDY 11

Medical history

My husband, Stephen Carroll, was diagnosed with bowel cancer in 2015. It took a long time to diagnose, but an attempt at major surgery was abandoned, because when they opened him up, the cancer was found to be dotted all over the abdominal cavity, so they created a stoma instead. Stephen was told that although his cancer was incurable, he could live with it for several years. He resolved to make the best of it, and many people, including medical staff, remarked over the years how cheerful and positive he was.

Progression

Stephen had regular bouts of chemotherapy to keep the cancer under control. At one stage there was a small spread to the liver, which was cleared up by chemotherapy. He suffered regular infections which resulted in hospital stays ranging from 3 to 11 days over the next couple of years, approximately once every two months, although he was never neutropenic (having low levels of white blood cells). He was always treated at Stoke Mandeville Hospital for these infections, and we found the doctors there were always positive in dealing with him.

Final stage

In January 2018, Stephen became ill and was vomiting constantly. A nurse advised him to go to Willen Hospice to attempt to get the vomiting under control. However, none of the medication they gave him stopped the vomiting. At first, he was eating and drinking, but he became less able to eat, and was barely taking spoonfuls of food. I asked about giving him intravenous fluids. A nurse told me they didn't do that. I spoke to one of the doctors, who was reluctant too. When I said it won't do him any harm, she agreed with me. So a saline drip was given, one bag over 12 hours. I also asked about feeding him if he was unable to eat. The doctors spoke to his oncologist at Stoke Mandeville Hospital who advised against it. We were not party to that conversation, so didn't get the opportunity to question it. We were told this on a Friday.

The next day the saline drip wasn't in place, so I asked for it to be reinstated. The doctor told me it had stopped working at 4am, so had been taken down. I was often told that the cannula (tube) could come out or his veins could collapse, so the drip would not work. I pointed out that he was given it at 4pm the previous day, so it would have stopped by 4am. She said she would check the notes. She explained to me that a drip was unnecessary and that the patient didn't need it. I said it wouldn't do him harm, and asked them to reinstate it. A nurse spoke to me, explaining how some complication could occur if a drip went the wrong way. I said that surely there would be observable signs if something like that happened, a point she accepted. She asked me if I'd like a doctor to come and explain it to me again. I declined this offer and decided to stay overnight with Stephen at that point.

On the Sunday morning, a doctor came in and spoke to me in a passive-aggressive manner, asking how long I expected them to keep giving him the drip, because it was a waste of time, and was just exchanging blood for water. I asked him where the blood was going then, and he said no new blood cells were being made. I replied that Stephen wasn't dying when he went into the hospice but he was now, and I would rather he died of cancer than of dehydration. The drip continued. Early on Monday morning, Stephen died. The drip was still running perfectly until then.

I left the hospice immediately after Stephen's body was collected. I didn't want to talk to any of the staff because I felt they had made Stephen's last days more stressful and difficult. I didn't write to them or express my complaints because I felt very emotional about it and I needed time to calm down and come to terms with his death. In the end, I did not contact them at all.

Medical opinion of Professor Ahmedzai

1. The 3-year time course of Stephen's illness – helped of course by his good tolerance of chemotherapy – was actually very good and reflects a high standard of oncology care.

2. In contrast, the care given by the hospice from the outset seems to be below the standards one would expect of a specialist palliative care service. Persistent vomiting would usually arise in such a case from bowel or gastric obstruction and I would expect the staff at a hospice to be capable of first diagnosing, and then palliating the distressing symptoms with success.

First, I would like to know whether the vomiting ever actually stopped, because in my experience there is a large range of medications and also non-pharmacological approaches such as acupuncture used in palliative care, which can alleviate vomiting.

Furthermore, did they consider placing a tube into the stomach via the nose to drain what fluid there was in his stomach? That would be a good approach and standard in any NHS hospital; in my experience nasogastric tubes are also offered in hospices.

3. Second, I find the hospice's attitudes and action with respect to the family's very reasonable requests for clinically assisted hydration (CAH) to be crass, ignorant and could be seen as negligent. Admittedly, such resistance to starting CAH used to be quite standard in UK hospices before and especially during the use of LCP. NICE guideline NG31 (see Appendix 3) clearly stated that a trial of assisted fluids could be tried if the patient and/or family requested it and there was no clear medical contraindication (i.e. a pre-existing condition or current treatment which would prevent the use of assisted fluids). I am unaware of the latter here, from the description.

Moreover, GMC guidance from 2010 is apposite here in recommending that the dying patient's wish for hydration (or of those close to the patient) "will usually be the deciding factor" (see Appendix 4). I am therefore moved to consider the hospice's actions to be negligent in this patient's care; and it is possible to argue that his death, while inevitable because of the advanced stage of his cancer, was possibly accelerated and more likely than not, made more unpleasant by their reluctance to adhere promptly to these guidelines.

4. It appears that once the hospice relented and started clinically assisted hydration, it embarked on intravenous fluids. Arguments were offered about the dangers of this approach. The alternative method – subcutaneous delivery – which is very well documented in the palliative care literature, is actually easier and safer in a hospice situation.

I admired Stephen's wife sticking to her requests for hydration and although we are not told, I would suspect his last two days were more comfortable. The manner of the doctor who was arguing against assisted hydration appears to be rude, condescending and using nonsensical arguments such "exchanging blood for water". In my experience, this was typical of the intimidating and patronising practices used by medical (and often nursing) staff in the time of the LCP, to influence relatives to accept the withholding or withdrawal of assisted hydration. It is now unacceptable and, in my opinion, could be considered negligent practice in the light of NICE guideline NG31 and the GMC 2010 guidance.

5. After Stephen's body was removed from the hospice, his wife's decision never to return or to lodge a complaint is a sad, but quite understandable reaction. Many families who are upset by the end of life care they see are reluctant or intimidated about raising their concerns or raising a complaint. On the contrary here, I would have expected a specialist palliative care service such as a hospice to take the initiative and reach out to the family after a reasonable time and offer to discuss the care with them. The absence of such an offer would reflect a very poor standard of bereavement care from this hospice.

CASE STUDY 12

The GPs at the surgery left my elderly mother in pain with undiagnosed gastric cancer. They refused to refer her to an oncologist or specialist and despite my protests, they claimed I agreed, which is untrue.

They made a decision that it was clinically inappropriate to investigate her condition, a decision not conveyed to me formally in writing, which would have allowed me to challenge it.

Dehydration

My mother was prone to dehydration due to her dysphagia (difficulty in swallowing). Several weeks before her death, a doctor from the surgery asked for blood tests to be done. I specifically wanted to know whether she was dehydrated but never got an answer from the doctors.

I believe there were huge failures by the surgery, and they breached their duty of care towards my mother. One doctor at the surgery agreed to refer my mother to hospital, following a second opinion request in July 2016, but on leaving the house, said "I will have to run it past her GP first", which I thought was unacceptable because it was that GP whose position I wanted a second opinion on.

Pain management

There was no cohesive care or pain management plan in place in my view and not enough reviews of her current medication, one of which was unsuitable (Depakote)[1] due to her dementia diagnosis. When she started use of Depakote in 2005, she said it did not agree with her. This drug can cause insomnia and she was in pain at night.

Hospital complaint

After my mother went into hospital in October 2016, I met with my representative from a mental health charity and a medical consultant on 28th October 2016. On that day, the issue of her abdominal pain was raised. The consultant's actual words were "If it was anything serious she would have succumbed to it by now". It was indeed something serious – gastric cancer – and she did eventually succumb to it.

DNACPR

Having had previous discussions with her GP about DNAR, a doctor from a surgery in Shevington, Wigan, wanted to put my mother on DNAR as part of her care plan, as documented in the GP records dated 3rd October 2016. On 7th October, a junior doctor at the Medical Admissions Unit (MAU) at Wigan Infirmary made it clear he wanted to put my mother on DNAR. I told him in no uncertain terms that I would not sign it. This was two days after her admission into hospital, when my mother was in the MAU at Wigan Infirmary. I was under pressure to sign the DNAR for my mother but I refused.

On 13th March 2018 on Lowton Ward, Wigan Infirmary, in a meeting with a doctor, I was told that they had decided not to resuscitate my mother if her heart stopped. I said that I disagreed with this decision. In June 2020, I got a further response from Wigan Infirmary about the DNAR. The letter spoke about "after previously agreeing a DNAR on my father" (words I had never spoken). I requested that this letter be amended, which was indeed done.

During my mother's last week in hospital, I had difficulty accessing information about her condition. This was 15th March 2018, one day before her death. I asked the hospital consultant about her condition, only to be dismissed by him, when he said he was too busy to speak to me. It seems to me that there was an agenda to bring her life to a close.

Diagnosis

She was admitted on 9th March 2018 to A&E at Wigan Infirmary, with possible retention, but this was later ruled out by the A&E urologist, following a bladder scan. This showed 900ml of possible ascites fluid. The doctors were questioning what had caused ascites (build-up of fluid within the abdomen). She had possible cirrhosis as the cause of this. She also had stage 1 acute kidney infection.

When I asked the physician what had caused her sudden deterioration, he said that ascites fluid was compressing her organs and she would die shortly. I was in total shock. Later, the hospital response stated her death was not as a direct result of the ascites, so what did cause it?

Coroner conversations

On leaving Wigan Infirmary on the day of her death, I spoke to a lady at Bolton Coroner's Office, stating that I believed something might have been administered to my mother before she died. She said that she had spoken to some of the doctors at the hospital and they had suspected it was cancer. Doctors never discussed this with me.

She also advised me to consider whether I wanted an ordinary post-mortem or an independent one, and to think it over. I settled on an independent one but didn't know how to proceed with it further. I was offered no guidance. I went to a hospital pathologist and asked for a toxicology test to be done. I was told that a pathologist would not do a toxicology test as part of the post-mortem, which I was not happy about.

On accessing my mother's medical records months later, I found a reference to midazolam prn, which was prescribed by a locum consultant. In the hospital's final response dated 31st January 2019, it indicated that there were three other medications present: morphine sulphate, glycopyrronium bromide and levomepromazepine. These were prescribed but it is unknown whether they were given. A toxicology test would have confirmed whether these medications were given or not. I believe the pathologist at Wigan Infirmary should have done a toxicology test to rule out which, if any, of the forementioned drugs were in her bloodstream before she died at the age of 94.

Medical opinion of Professor Ahmedzai

1. This is a sad case spanning nearly two years, of a 94-year-old lady who had abdominal symptoms that went largely un-investigated and finally when a diagnosis of gastric (stomach) cancer was made, it was too late to give any meaningful treatment.

2. In my opinion it was extremely unlikely that the patient had gastric cancer in October 2106 and lived till March 2018. The usual prognosis for this cancer, without anti-cancer treatment, is 3-6 months. However, I cannot dispute that she may have died of gastric cancer in the end, as she had evidence of abdominal ascites which is common with this cancer. However, we are told that she also had liver cirrhosis, which can independently cause ascites.

3. The handling of the DNACPR discussions leaves a lot to be desired in terms of communication and patient/family-oriented decision-making. This, and the alleged refusal of the consultant to talk to the son, would be in breach of NICE guideline NG31 (2015, see Appendix 3), which recommends open discussion including family for such decisions. Specifically, recommendation 1.2.1:

"Establish the communication needs and expectations of people who may be entering their last days of life, taking into account: if they would like a person important to them to be present when making decisions about their care; their current level of understanding that they may be nearing death; their cognitive status and if they have any specific speech, language or other communication needs; how much information they would like to have about their prognosis; any cultural, religious, social or spiritual needs or preferences."

In my opinion, on the evidence available to me, the medical practitioners in primary care and especially in the hospital, had failed in their duty of care to follow these recommendations.

However I have to add that the DNACPR was probably clinically irrelevant in this case, because the mode of death was unlikely to be primarily cardiac. However, this does not appear to have been explained to the family, which again could be seen as a failure of communication.

4. The patient's son was concerned that it appeared four drugs were prescribed for his mother near the end of life: midazolam, morphine sulphate, glycopyrronium bromide and levomepromazepine. The first, midazolam, is a benzodiazepine sedative that from one of the hospital documents I was shown was prescribed "PRN" meaning "as required"; its purpose was to replace the anti-epileptic drug sodium valproate (Depakote) which the patient had previously been taking. (From the information I have been supplied, I cannot see the indication for the Depakote to be prescribed. In an older person with dementia, its long-term use should be reviewed and probably reduced or discontinued.)

It was not clear to the son whether these prescribed drugs had actually been given. It is quite possible that they were, because it may be hard for a lay person to read handwritten drug charts. Regrettably, these charts were not made available to me.

I should note that the four drugs are all commonly used at the end of life to manage different symptoms that could be distressing to dying people. Under the now abolished LCP, they were often all prescribed together in a "blanket" fashion, and that made it easier for busy or inexperienced nurses to give them unquestioningly and that could cause unnecessary sedation, possibly accelerating the death. NICE guideline NG31 made it quite clear that this practice must stop and although any of these drugs could be used, they must be prescribed on an individually justified basis.

I therefore believe the son's questions about these drugs are legitimate and should have been answered by the hospital and the autopsy with toxicology reports. If they showed that the drugs had been used blanket-fashion as with the LCP, a case could be made for there being an act of clinical negligence.

5. The distress caused to the son on the question of which drugs were administered to his mother in the last admission would have been quite avoidable with better communication from the hospital team, as recommended by NICE NG31. I also found the reported attitudes of the coroner's office and of the pathologist who performed the autopsy in refusing to check for blood levels of sedative drugs were, respectively, unhelpful and callous. It would have been easy to perform these tests in order to allay the concerns of a distressed relative. However, I am unable to say that these alleged actions or omissions were negligent or breached the doctors' duty of care.

------

1 Depakote is sodium valproate, which is an anti-epileptic drug.

CASE STUDY 13

In 2019 my father was diagnosed with dementia. In February 2020, my father moved into a Carlisle care home. It soon became apparent that there seemed to be an ethos of sedating residents. Twenty weeks later he was dead. Initially, it seemed too easy for GP X to prescribe strong antipsychotics to my father behind closed doors during lockdown. It also felt like GP X's relationship with the care home manager and owner was too comfortable.

The medications that were prescribed to my father since his diagnosis did not seem to be necessary. They seemed to lead to more medications being needed. I now understand that these medications – sertraline, fludrocortisone, risperidone, a salbutamol inhaler, and nitrofurantoin – all contributed to the shortening of his life. All of these were administered in the weeks and days leading up to his death, and depleted his potassium levels and caused dehydration and urinary tract infections.

Father's last week

On 17th June 2020, I expressed my concerns after seeing my father face to face in our only garden visit. He was breathless. On 21st June, he was still the same. The care home management played down my concerns and said it was only a dip in my father's dementia. I felt helpless and had to intervene, so I handed a letter to the surgery, insisting the risperidone be stopped. I was against the prescription from the outset.

On the 23rd June, I had a 30-minute phone chat with my father after lunch. He was coherent and not in pain, just breathless. He asked about when I would have his home safe for his return. My father's gas boiler and electrics were in need of updating. It would not have been possible to do this whilst my father was living in the property.

Later that day blood samples were finally taken. The diagnosis was hypokalaemia (low potassium). GP X subsequently recommended a diet of bananas, tomato juice and a potassium replacement (which, according to charts, was never given). My father was eating normally that day according to the food and fluids charts, but the care home manager administered lorazepam to treat the symptoms of the hypokalaemia! I believe that GP X could have saved my father's life that day with a potassium drip.

Father's last days

On June 24th, I was briefly ushered in to see my father. They had sedated him. This treatment only masked the agitation caused by hypokalaemia, and it felt wrong that I could not communicate with him. I asked to stay but they refused. Suddenly my father had a flash of consciousness and asked where I was going. He was obviously sedated but aware.

Later, GP X phoned. He said that the damage was done and my father was at end of life. This seemed incomprehensible. He had been eating and chatting the day before.

On June 24th and 25th, I was allowed to sit with my father. Midazolam and morphine were being administered by a syringe driver. I wiped his mouth with a small sponge. He was permitted one visitor. As his only child, I felt very alone. I felt like I was watching him being put down like an animal. It felt wrong. What effort had been made to save him? I did not understand what weeks of low potassium had done to his organs. I felt railroaded.

My wonderful father passed away when I briefly went home. Nothing felt right. It seemed like care home staff, the GP and nurses were playing God. It felt like his death was avoidable.

Questions about due process

I have since looked at all my father's records, and it seems that there had never been a review of his medications, several of which can lead to low potassium and even death.

I also discovered that my father had been effectively imprisoned in the care home against his wishes, because the Deprivation of Liberty Safeguards process had not been properly followed. Even the Do Not Attempt Resuscitation documentation had been signed on 6th February 2020 without my knowledge, even though I had lasting power of attorney.

On 26th June 2020, GP X wanted my agreement on the cause of death, i.e. elderly with dementia. Concerned, I contacted the coroner. The eventual result of the autopsy was ischaemic heart failure, despite my father not having any history of heart problems. Sadly, my father never returned home despite the works being completed because he died that day. I understood my father's death was hastened by the over-use of antipsychotics that were administered against my wishes or without discussion. I felt I was being railroaded throughout the process without my having the knowledge to stop it happening.

I have complained to the care home, doctor, social services, the CQC and my MP. I also wrote a letter to the Ombudsman which I never sent, as I was dealing with my own grief. All the medical documents are currently with my lawyer.

Medical opinion of Professor Ahmedzai

1. This patient is said to have been diagnosed with dementia. It is not clear who made this diagnosis and whether it was verified. It would have been helpful to know what the symptoms and signs during 2019 to February 2020 were. Some features of his history in 2020 could be in keeping with this diagnosis. However, the number of drugs he is said to have received for the dementia is worrying, because it is not clear to me whether these were for dementia, agitation or other indications.

2. The medication I am most concerned about is fludrocortisone. This is a hormone replacement medicine used when the body is not producing enough of its own adrenal gland hormones (commonly known as steroids). The commonest use is for a condition known as Addison's disease, in which the adrenal glands fail to produce these steroid hormones. It seems that the daughter was not aware of this condition.

Fludrocortisone has no indication for use in dementia and indeed one of its known side-effects is mental changes including agitation. In my opinion it is almost certainly the cause of his low potassium. Anyone on regular fludrocortisone for a valid reason should have regular blood monitoring for potassium, of which a GP should be mindful.

The electronic medicines compendium (emc)[1] is a standard source of data on all UK medication. It states that among the known neurological side-effects of fludrocortisone are:

"euphoria, psychological dependence, depression, insomnia, convulsions, increased intracranial pressure with papilloedema (pseudo-tumour cerebri) usually after treatment, vertigo, headache, neuritis or paraesthesias and aggravation of pre-existing psychiatric conditions and epilepsy.

A wide range of psychiatric reactions including affective disorders (such as irritable, euphoric, depressed and labile mood, and suicidal thoughts), psychotic reactions (including mania, delusions, hallucinations, and aggravation of schizophrenia), behavioural disturbances, irritability, anxiety, sleep disturbances, and cognitive dysfunction including confusion and amnesia have been reported."

Other serious side-effects include:

"sodium retention, fluid retention, congestive heart failure in susceptible patients, potassium loss, cardiac arrhythmias or ECG changes due to potassium deficiency."

It could thus lead to cardiac rhythm disorders – some of which could cause a cardiac arrest which could potentially be managed by cardiopulmonary resuscitation (CPR). In my opinion, prescription of fludrocortisone, without a clear reason (at least not known to his next of kin) and without evidence of regular blood monitoring for low potassium, is likely, on the balance of probabilities, to have contributed to his death. In the apparent absence of evidence of blood monitoring, this would lead me to suspect the GP of a seriously negligent breach of his duty of care.

3. The care home was apparently following the GP's prescription of medications but should have been alerted to the multiple potential side-effects listed above, arising from his fludrocortisone (and possibly his other anti-psychotic medication). The known side-effects of agitation and convulsions could possibly be masked by sedative drugs such as lorazepam and midazolam; but these drugs are certainly not indicated for low potassium.

Thus the use of sedative drugs such as lorazepam in this context was highly risky and could have contributed to his deterioration. However, it is not clear whether this use was on the instructions of the GP; if it was, it would be further evidence of the GP's serious breach of duty of care. Alternatively, it could point to a gross misjudgement of use of a resident's medication by the care home manager.

4. The daughter identifies two other aspects of her father's care which give me cause for concern. First, if he had been placed unilaterally on a Deprivation of Liberty (DOL) safeguard and without the family's knowledge, then this would appear to be in breach of the legal procedures laid down for a DOL application. I understand that this would be an unlawful act on behalf of the care home, with the possibility of legal damages and costs being obtained. With respect to the patient's welfare, in my opinion the alleged unlawful DOL represents an infringement of his human rights, but I cannot say how much this may have contributed to his death.

5. Second, as mentioned above, having the DNACPR signed without the knowledge of the relative with lasting power of attorney (LPA) was certainly in my opinion, unreasonable and disrespectful. A person holding LPA cannot insist on a particular treatment being given, but I understand he or she would normally have to be consulted on major medical decisions. Specifically I understand that failure to consult the Lasting Attorney on such a critical matter as CPR could be deemed unlawful.

6. Finally this case highlights the isolation that many people must have felt who watched loved ones admitted to care homes and hospitals and who then died largely alone, during the COVID-19 pandemic. The Care Quality Commission (CQC)[2] found that many older people in this situation were being placed unilaterally by GPs on DNACPR orders during the pandemic. It is fair to point out that in most cases a DNACPR would not make a difference, because the mode of death would not respond to CPR. However, in this case as I have pointed out, the hypokalaemia could have led to a terminal cardiac arrest, and in my opinion that could have responded successfully to CPR and emergency paramedic and hospital attention.

---

[1] https://www.medicines.org.uk/emc/product/12168/smpc

[2] *Blanket 'do not resuscitate' orders imposed on English care homes, finds CQC.* The Guardian, 18 March 2021. https://www.theguardian.com/society/2021/mar/18/blanket-do-not-resuscitate-orders-imposed-on-english-care-homes-finds-cqc

CASE STUDY 14

Routine renal dialysis appointment

My father had Type 1 diabetes and end stage renal failure. He had regular dialysis and was considered for a renal transplant one month before his death aged 47.

On 18th December 2020, he went for renal dialysis. He had to be taken off the machine early, as he had vomited and felt dizzy. This wasn't unusual, as he often suffered with vertigo during dialysis, but once he came home, he was fine.

Problems with condition

Four days later, he otherwise seemed fine but became tired in the evening, sleeping intermittently, saying he was nauseous, felt cold and "off" and believed he had a bug or virus. He rang the renal unit, asking for his COVID-19 result. It was negative. He woke in a confused state and complained that he couldn't see. We rang an ambulance. His observations were checked and found to be all right, apart from high blood sugars.

Hospital assurances with mixed messages

He was taken to Salford Royal Hospital. A doctor rang, saying that it was likely he would be in hospital for a few days, and that he would be moved out of A&E when a bed became available in the renal ward. Every time we called the ward, we were told he was okay. On 24th December, a nurse told us that they had had difficulty rousing Mr Sharp in the morning and were getting quite concerned but that "he's absolutely fine, sat up having a cup of tea".

On Christmas Day morning, we rang the ward again, and were told that Dad was doing well. Around 2pm, we were told he was okay and was on dialysis but didn't know his date of birth. As a family, we were concerned and some of us decided we'd take some belongings up to Dad. We were told: "We've been trying to get hold of you. Mr Sharp is unwell, he's struggling with breathing and we're concerned about his heart." In fact, nobody had contacted us.

When in the ward, I pleaded with a nurse to let me see Dad. She agreed but said I could only see him for a minute. I was given PPE. When seeing Dad, I was absolutely shocked. This wasn't the same Dad who had walked out of the house into an ambulance 48 hours earlier. He didn't know I was there. I shouted, "Dad, Dad, it's me". His eyes were all over the place, his lips were dropping and his speech was slurred.

Questions with unsatisfactory answers

I questioned why Dad wasn't aware of who I was or that I was there. The nurse answered that he probably just had an infection and then left the room. I made further enquiries. Dad was now being moved to the heart care unit for cardiac monitoring. When I asked whether Dad was going to be okay, I was assured that he was going to be fine. I should never have left.

On arrival at home a call came, saying that Dad had deteriorated and that consultants from the Intensive Care Unit (ICU) and High Care Unit (HCU) were on the way to review him. A later call informed us that after an assessment, he didn't require ICU and was now being transferred to HCU, as originally planned.

We phoned again, and were told his breathing was quite erratic. A nurse said she would wait 30 minutes to see if his breathing settled. If it didn't, she'd have to bleep the doctors to review him. Another follow-up call informed us that he had deteriorated again and he was now being relocated to ICU.

We then spoke to an ICU doctor who said Dad needed help with his breathing and "needed a line put in", but without further explanation. Dad was taken to ICU. A few hours later, Mum was phoned by an ICU doctor who asked many questions: how active Dad was at home, how he got to and from dialysis, whether he could manage stairs, whether he was fully independent. Mum answered "Yes" to every question. The doctor said: "We don't know where to go from here." My mum asked whether this meant that he was dying. He said, "Unfortunately, I think he is dying".

We shot to the hospital, finding Dad already unconscious. He died at 6.30am. We had no idea what was given as cause of death, being told: "Due to Christmas, if it needed passing to the Coroner, it would delay things." It was never passed to the Coroner. When we complained, seeking answers about the cause of Dad's death, we were informed that he had been treated for sepsis of an unknown origin, but this wasn't previously mentioned.

Family excluded from decisions

Medical records show that Dad was being treated for a suspected infection, his chest became worse and his liver function tests had started to become abnormal on Christmas Day, while his liver had started to fail too. He was said to lack mental capacity. None of this information was given to us. His cause of death was listed as congestive cardiac failure, which we questioned, asking what had caused his heart to fail. The cause was said to be unclear, either a heart attack or an infection of the heart valve, and we were informed that his liver had begun to fail and that further resuscitation was felt to be inappropriate.

Dad was said to have had underlying health conditions. We contacted our local Coroner with our concerns surrounding his death. An investigation was carried out but nothing happened. We discovered that Dad had had unwitnessed falls and that he had been found on the floor, but we were never informed about this. Medical records also say that Dad became confused, delirious, agitated and ripped his own cannula out. We weren't told how much he was suffering, but instead were led to believe he was fine.

We have discovered that a DNAR had been put in place, but this was never discussed with us, despite records stating the exact contrary. We would never have agreed to this.

Medical opinion of Professor Ahmedzai

1. This is a distressing case study, rather different from many others in this Report, because it centres on a relatively young person who had known chronic conditions (kidney failure and diabetes) but who had recently been thought to be fit enough for a kidney transplant, but then died acutely in hospital on Boxing Day in unexplained circumstances, and without his family present.

2. Coupled with the difficulty in rousing him the previous morning, the patient not knowing his date of birth should have been a warning to the staff that (a) he might be becoming confused or delirious from an acute event (infection, stroke, cardiac, etc); and (b) the family should immediately be placed on alert and ideally called in. Of course there is the understandable complicating factor of COVID-related restrictions in hospitals at that time. However, it would have been reasonable to invite one member of the family, both to inform the family of the change and also to help give the father comfort. It is well known that one of the best remedies for acute delirium is to enable the patient to interact with familiar people.

The daughter tells us that the ward stated it had been trying to contact them, but it is concerning that the family did not know of this. Often in practice, although there is an identified need to phone relatives, because of the ward being very busy and with staff shortages (both factors in the pandemic), the call is never made, which may have happened in this case.

3. The rapidly changing events of Christmas Day evening and the phone call from the ICU doctor indicate that the father was now clearly gravely ill. Again, we understand that the pandemic was placing restrictions on hospital staff time and also capacity to bring in relatives. However, I find it to be rather poor communication from the ICU doctor to hold a detailed phone conversation asking searching questions (the answers to many of which should already have been part of his renal department records), before ending with "Unfortunately, I think he is dying".

It would have been kinder and more helpful to the family to have been given that news gently at the beginning, with the request for someone to come to the hospital as soon as possible. This is poor communication practice in the case of a gravely ill patient, highlighted by NICE guideline NG31, recommendation 1.2 (see Appendix 3), but does not in my opinion, in itself represent a seriously negligent breach of care.

4. The information the family was given immediately after the patient's death regarding the potential "delay" from notifying the Coroner of this acute, unexpected – and as far as we know, unexplained – death, is far from satisfactory.

First, the death of any person in hospital around Christmas is bound to be tied up in delays regarding notification and movement of the deceased, etc. It was unhelpful and misleading to suggest to the family that referring to the Coroner at this time would cause a delay.

Second, if there is any suspicion of an unexplained death, it is the duty of attending doctors or their senior in line, to notify the Coroner's office and leave a message (The Notification of Deaths Regulations 2019, see Appendix 6).

This states:

"Circumstances in which the duty to notify arises...

Section 3.—(1) The circumstances are ...

b) the registered medical practitioner suspects that the person's death was unnatural but does not fall within any of the circumstances listed in sub-paragraph (a);

and

(c) the registered medical practitioner...

(i) is an attending medical practitioner required to sign a certificate of cause of death in relation to the deceased person; but

(ii) despite taking reasonable steps to determine the cause of death, considers that the cause of death is unknown"

Section 4-1 states that:

"A registered medical practitioner who must notify a relevant senior coroner of a person's death under regulation 2(1) must do so as soon as is reasonably practicable after the duty arises."

Thus, in my opinion the doctors advising the family appear to have failed in their legal responsibility with respect to the 2019 Regulations to notify the Coroner of an unexplained or suspicious death; and not to do it immediately. Furthermore these omissions, if verified, amounted to failure of care of the family after the patient's death.

5. It seems clear from the daughter's account that the hospital must have been aware from Christmas Eve, if not Christmas Day itself, that the father was deteriorating rapidly and in an unexplained and thus unpredictable way. Learning that the hospital concluded at around this time that the patient had lost mental capacity, I think this should have led immediately to the family being called in for a discussion about medical decision-making and his preferences – and possibly leading to a 'Best Interests' meeting. Once again, this apparent inaction is in not in keeping with NICE guidance NG31 section 1.2. The hospital staff should have asked whether he had given someone Lasting Power of Attorney for medical decisions, and asked that person to come in.

Of course, it is sad and understandable to reflect that the impact of the COVID-19 pandemic will have contributed strongly to the hospital failing to do these routine things, but the fact remains that his medical care at this point appears to have fallen below the standard of practice. His human rights were also breached because of the staff's apparent failure to attempt to engage the family in "best interests" decision-making.

6. From a medical point of view, I could sympathise with the hospital team in declaring that "congestive cardiac failure" was a contributing factor. But as a physician I still would support the family's questions as to why the patient had gone into heart failure. It is evident that the hospital staff did not know: again, this points to the need and medical obligation to refer the death to the Coroner. The staff would appear to have failed in this duty with respect to The Notification of Deaths Regulations 2019.

7. It appears that the family, very reasonably, contacted the Coroner's office unilaterally and as a result, they learned more about the events that befell the father before his death. Their late finding of "unwitnessed falls" that had not been previously shared with the family is, in my opinion, unforgivable and would represent a further breach of duty of care towards them as responsible adults for a person who had acutely lost mental capacity.

8. The cause of death shared with the family was "congestive cardiac failure". Learning that the hospital had placed the patient on a DNACPR order without informing the family is sadly not surprising, but seems clearly wrong to me for two reasons.

First, my impression from the daughter's account is that he probably did not have a significant heart problem before this admission. If he did and it was likely to be major, then I strongly doubt that he would have been accepted for the renal transplant just a month previously. So in my opinion, this was an unforeseen acute cardiac event which I am aware is not uncommon in renal failure patients, but in the absence of information to the family, should have been assumed to be a potentially treatable condition.

Among the reasons why the heart can stop suddenly in such a person is rapidly changing imbalances in blood chemicals (serum electrolytes such as potassium), mainly because the kidneys would be unable to respond to them. I would defer to a cardiologist, but my understanding is that in these circumstances, CPR with intensive electrolyte management stands a good chance of re-starting the heart; as successfully, perhaps, as from a major "heart attack" following a coronary thrombosis. For this reason, in my opinion it is indefensible that a DNACPR decision was made at all.

Second, this is precisely the scenario in which it would have been imperative to consult the family members, especially if one held Lasting Power of Attorney, preferably face-to-face, but in the context of the rapid changes and the pandemic restrictions, at least over the phone.

Again, I am not an expert in renal medicine or acute cardiac care, but in my opinion as an experienced physician with expertise in end of life decision-making, the hospital staff appear to have seriously failed the patient in this respect. The eventual outcome may have been the same, i.e. he may have died from overwhelming sepsis or a major coronary attack, so I cannot say that the DNACPR decision could have contributed to his death; but conversely, I think it is reasonable to advise the family that if he had received CPR, he may have stood a better chance of surviving this acute event.

This is precisely why, in my opinion, a Coroner could have demanded an autopsy and carried out a formal inquest.

WHEN 'END OF LIFE CARE' GOES WRONG

CASE STUDY 15

My mother, Magdalen Boyle, died at home in Ivybridge, Devon on April 25th 2021.

Overview

Magdalen was diagnosed with small cell lung cancer in December 2019, which had metastasized to her brain by January 2021. By April 2020, my mum had undergone five rounds of chemotherapy. By February 2021 she had had an additional three sessions of radiation therapy. Palliative care was offered from March 2021. The healthcare workers were kind, thoughtful and hard-working in my mum's final weeks at home. However, the communication from lead medical professionals was shockingly poor, with Katie (my mother's daughter-in-law) and I not knowing what to expect in those final weeks. My mother's care fell short of being in her best interests. Katie and I made a formal complaint to St Luke's Hospice shortly after my mother's death. We received a response promptly, but there was no acceptance of failings – particularly in relation to the CQC's fundamental standards for care, regarding which we had highlighted failings in the facilitation of Magdalen's care in terms of Person-centred care, Consent and Duty of candour.

No care plan

Magdalen chose to receive palliative care at home. Katie and I supported Mum in this decision. The Oncology Support Team identified St Luke's Hospice Community Team as being best suited to supporting Mum at home. We learned just days before Mum died that there was no care plan in place. And following Mum's death, we learned that a verbal care plan had been assumed. In their response to our complaint, St. Luke's stated, "We wouldn't typically have a written care plan within this St. Luke's team". However we found it unsatisfactory that there was no explanation as to why a clear and informative discussion hadn't been offered to my mum or ourselves, informing her of what medical treatments she could expect in her closing days. This would have given us the opportunity to explore treatments and make decisions with respect to her ethical and religious views - particularly Mum's views on dehydration and starvation whilst under heavy sedation.

Expectations in care

At no point was a discussion entered into about what would happen when my mum deteriorated and what drugs might be considered or required. This is something the NHS website states should be one of the 5 priorities for care.[1] Three of these priorities relevant to my mum include:

"The staff involved in your care should talk sensitively and honestly to you and the people close to you; You and the people close to you should be involved in decisions about how you are treated and cared for, if this is what you want; and An individual plan of care should be agreed with you and delivered with compassion."

Lack of consent

Without such communication, it is impossible for St Luke's to have gained Mum's informed consent. So when a change in medication rendered Mum unconscious and unable to communicate in her last days of life, her wishes and feelings in relation to her treatment were not known. It was only our researching the drugs (and particularly the drug combination) that alerted us to a medical protocol known as the Liverpool Care Pathway, that we were hitherto unaware of. Knowing my mother, I feel confident that had she been informed what the combination of drugs would do to her, she would not have consented to this treatment.

Sedating drugs

Mum, Katie and myself were not informed of the nature of the three drugs contained within the syringe driver used in her last few days. A family member who is a registered nurse remarked that my mum looked "out of it" compared with the day before the syringe driver was started, when Mum was engaging in conversation. Understanding that the morphine was responsible for this change, I made the decision (as Mum could now neither consent nor decline any treatment) to remove the morphine from the driver. The following day, Mum was a little more aware and able to whisper, but she could not open her eyes at all. It was clear that Mum was not anywhere near as aware as she had been before the syringe driver was used. By Friday 23rd April, I discovered that midazolam was also being administered to her via the syringe driver for heavy sedation.

Throughout our experience with St Luke's and the community nursing team, our overall impression was that they were following a pathway or plan that was not shared with Mum or ourselves. It ultimately rendered her unconscious, which was against her wishes. We were repeatedly told that Mum was "peaceful and settled" by staff who visited the house, but we felt she was sedated to facilitate easier care by an overstretched workforce.

Medical opinion of Professor Ahmedzai

1. Small cell lung cancer with brain metastases has a predictable time course and there would have been ample time to plan and coordinate her care between the oncologists, GP and hospice (community) team. I found the timing of palliative care involvement to be very late – two months after Magdalen had developed brain disease. Although this appears to have worked for the weeks before Magdalen's death, the family still felt that communication was lacking in the decision-making – especially regarding end of life drugs – during her last days.

Having seen the response from the Nurse consultant of St Luke's Hospice, it is clear to me that the hospice team acknowledges the communication regarding the medication and use of the syringe driver in the last days fell below acceptable standards. Consequently, the Hospice has undertaken to review their communication systems.

2. The use of a syringe driver with triple medication has the hallmarks of the old LCP, but this had already been abolished eight years before her death. Having seen the Hospice's written response, I can understand the reasoning for including the midazolam (replacement for oral Keppra that she had been taking to prevent epileptic fits); and for the morphine (reports of distress and pain which the introduction of morphine appeared to relieve).

In addition, the nursing team have documented that when they removed the morphine at the request of the family, Magdalen experienced more pain and had told them she preferred to be more sedated than experience pain and so it was re-started. This would meet the standard of care at end of life. However, I can find no record of the third drug or its justification.

3. Magdalen's family were concerned at the lack of a written care plan, and having read the hospice's response I concur that this was unacceptable. I have yet to see a palliative care service which denies the use of written care plans on the grounds that the situation may change. The hospice would need to prove that that they had individualised care plans in place (whether written or not) and that they were following these. These should have included records of communication with the patient and family. In failing to keep written care plans, the hospice community team appears to be in breach of current end of life care NICE guideline (NG31, 2015) and its associated quality standard (QS144, 2017).

QS144 states very clearly:

"Quality statements
Adults in the last days of life, and the people important to them, are given opportunities to discuss, develop and review an individualised care plan.

"Rationale
Care at the end of life should be responsive to the personal needs and preferences of the person who is dying. Discussions with the person can identify any existing expressed preferences for care, such as advance care plans, and explore their goals and wishes, preferred care setting, current and anticipated care needs and any cultural, religious or social preferences. This information will be captured in an individualised care plan. Opportunities for discussion should continue to be given so the plan can reflect any changes in the person's wishes or needs in the last days of their life."

Thus NICE policy which had been published four years before Magdalen's death was very clear that she should have had a care plan, specifically so that it could be discussed and amended as her condition changed. In my opinion, the admitted failure of St Luke's Hospice team to have such a procedure represents a serious breach of their duty of care, for which the hospice management should be held corporately responsible.

4. The use of heavy sedation, without good justification, is unacceptable, especially if it shown that there were shortages of community staff. Regardless of staffing levels, she should have been reviewed and sedation should have been minimised in order to allow Magdalen to have communication with her family.

5. The assertion of dehydration and starvation are serious and the hospice team should have reasons for withholding feeding and hydration. NICE guideline NG31 (see Appendix 3) is very clear on hydration and the need to offer oral fluids if acceptable to the patient; or else to consider a clinical trial of assisted hydration. The hospice response that giving intravenous fluids could carry a risk is unacceptable, because the alternative which is subcutaneous is actually easier and also safer, especially at home, in that respect. Once again, denying hydration has the hallmark of the old LCP practices that were abolished.

---

[1] https://www.nhs.uk/conditions/end-of-life-care/what-to-expect-from-care/

CASE STUDY 16

Medical history and care in the months leading up to my father's death

David suffered heart disease for 30 years. Until November 2019 he had had two-monthly check-ups with a cardiac specialist, to monitor medication dosage. He often instructed David that it was dangerous to stop taking Furosemide, a medication to control oedema (swollen tissue caused by build-up of fluid).

After November 2019, David had no cardiac check-ups. Two telephone appointments were cancelled. GP advice was to avoid prolonged sitting, to control the oedema.

On 26th July 2021, David attended the Friarage Hospital, to have fluid removed from his lungs to help with his breathing. His wife was not allowed to attend. The ten-minute procedure was successful, but David had to sit all day, while, according to my father, staff "tried to find someone who could carry out the procedure", despite the visit having been made by appointment. Oedema in David's limbs worsened from that day.

Admittance to hospital and the first two days

On Tuesday 31st August 2021, a doctor visited and ordered an ambulance for David. David's wife believed that David was being admitted to the Friarage to treat oedema in his scrotum, a simple procedure, similar to the one performed on 26th July. Again, she was told she could not attend. There was no indication that David's condition was serious. David walked into the ambulance and his wife expected him to be home that day or the following day.

On Wednesday 1st September, David's wife called the Friarage. In the conversation, no information was provided on his condition being serious, or that all treatment had been stopped. On Thursday 2nd September, David's son and one of two daughters were contacted by the Friarage and told that their father was dying. His wife was not contacted. When the family arrived, David was heavily sedated, his pyjamas were soaked in blood, his arm swollen and severely bruised. His entire body was oedematous.

The "Pathway"

The consultant told family that David had refused treatment and was "actively dying". The consultant had denied him fluid, nutrition and his usual medication, only administering pain-relief and oxygen. A nurse later told the family that this was called "The Pathway". Senior staff were not forthcoming on when David had been placed on the Pathway.

During a subsequent discussion, a consultant explained to the family that giving fluids, nutrition and medication would "prolong (David's) suffering", and a cannula and nutrition tube would cause discomfort. The family noticed a contradiction in this statement: if the pain of dehydration and starvation could be eased with pain-relief medication, why would this not be effective for pain caused by a cannula or nutrition tube?

Over the next four days, David was heavily sedated or in extreme pain, yet on occasion he became lucid and aware. At these times, he repeatedly asked when he was going home, read the time from the clock, and requested water and food. Family were told not to give him anything by mouth, as it could be dangerous.

Twice, when he was coherent, the family asked David if he wished to stop treatment. Both times he looked shocked and affirmed his wish to continue treatment.

Behaviour of senior staff

Our family disputed with senior staff that David would ask or wish to stop treatment. During an effort by family to video Dad's wishes to continue treatment, security was called, and the family's phone was confiscated.

Our family also repeatedly asked that David be given fluid and nutrition, which was refused. We stated several times to senior staff that we accepted David was dying but that he should not die of thirst and starvation. Behaviour of senior staff was aggressive and insensitive. David's wife was told on one occasion with a wagged finger that she "just had to accept her husband was dying".

Outcome

On Sunday 5th September, David's swallow was assessed, and he was given a small amount of fluid and food by mouth. On Monday, by 3pm, he had not been offered any food; the family had to request it. It was too little, too late.

That night he was awake and aware, repeatedly requesting food, which was not available. He suffered obvious immense pain despite being on a syringe driver for pain relief.

Later, we discovered that removing medication for heart failure from patients with chronic heart failure expedites decompensated heart failure and death. This was the cause of his death on Tuesday morning, as confirmed by the death certificate. He was 84.

Medical opinion of Professor Ahmedzai

1. This case study is a harrowing account of how a chronically ill person had a desperate end of his life that also traumatised his family. It is not clear to me why David's regular cardiac follow-ups were stopped, other than the pandemic starting in early 2020. Still, he could have had clinic appointments without his family present or have been reviewed via telephone calls, as we know became commonplace and very successful during the height of the pandemic. He could also have been offered cardiac nurse specialist follow-up at home, or again, by remote means.

2. In the absence of any further information, I must conclude that he was experiencing natural progression of his cardiac failure. But it is surprising that the family were not told that his medication was altered because it was clearly no longer controlling his condition. Drainage of what I presume was a cardiogenic pleural effusion (fluid gathering outside the lung as a result of heart failure) is not a routine procedure in a patient with chronic cardiac failure, and so I would have expected that the patient and ideally the family should have been informed that this now indicated his heart failure was progressing.

3. Oedema (soft but uncomfortable and unsightly swelling) of the lower part of the body, starting from the feet and ankles and creeping up to the genital area and eventually the lower half of the trunk, is a feature of progressive uncontrolled cardiac failure. It is what used to be called "dropsy" in the days before modern cardiac drugs. It begs the question of what changes the cardiologists were making to his heart failure drugs to keep up with this marked progression, and why they were not communicating these to him and his family.

4. The observation that he "walked into the ambulance" is not compatible, in my clinical experience, with a patient having such advanced cardiac failure that he might die in days. It suggests that something else influenced the doctors in the hospital to regard his disease as being "terminal" and thus change his goals of treatment.

However, it seems to me to be unusual and cruel for them to have decided that he was in a terminal decline and not to have shared this fully with the patient and family. If true, I suspect it would also represent poor cardiological practice and it certainly breaches the NICE NG31 guideline (see Appendix 3), published five and a half years previously, that makes recommendations (Appendix 3, section 1.2 Communication) to all clinicians to initiate end of life discussions and shared decision-making with patient and family, if they consider that the patient may soon die.

5. We are told that on the day after admission, there was no mention in the telephone call of his condition being gravely serious. Neither were they informed that his routine medication had been stopped, something that should have, in the circumstances, required consent from the patient and this being shared with the family. Only one day later were some family members (but strangely, not his wife) contacted by phone to be informed that he was now dying.

It is tempting for a layperson to imagine that the increasing oedema "from that day" (on the first hospital admission) was a consequence of his having to sit all day in the clinic or, later, lie in a hospital bed. However, I suspect it was actually much more serious, a sign of worsening cardiac failure, just as the pleural effusion was. Being in the middle of the COVID pandemic is no excuse for the hospital staff unilaterally withdrawing David's cardiac treatment, which in my opinion could be regarded as a breach of duty of care, which I suspect would not be defended by other physicians.

6. In my opinion, the description of the conversation the family had on the day they were called in, bears the hallmarks of the types of conversation carried out until seven years previously (mid-2014), when the Liverpool Care Pathway was still in use. In this case the family were informed – very late – that the father had been placed on an "end of life pathway".

Having been involved in submitting evidence to the LCP Review panel in 2013, I held subsequent meetings with its chair Baroness Neuberger over the following years, and we were aware that in some places there was reluctance to make the recommended changes and in reality, some places made merely cosmetic changes to the LCP wording. In spite of the *One Chance to Get it Right* report in 2014 (see Appendix 2) and the NICE guideline NG31 in 2015 (Appendix 3), we agreed that our intelligence was that some hospitals and other NHS care settings continued using basically the same blanket and tick-box approaches as prevailed under the LCP, but under a different name. Specifically, these settings made only feeble attempts to personalise care and individualise prescribing for people who were thought to be imminently dying.

Other hallmarks of the misuse of the LCP included: failure to gain consent from the patient for the change in direction of treatment; failure to inform families; active and rapid withdrawal of all or most previous medication; unjustified withholding of nutrition and hydration. My personal observation of these LCP and post-LCP continuing practices was that the cruellest example of clinical behaviour was when clinicians made a decision that someone was dying and refused to budge from that view, even days or sometimes weeks after the patient evidently did not die. Thus, the LCP came to be known as a "one-way" pathway.

NICE guideline NG31 explicitly recommended clinicians who were caring for a person who might be dying to review them at least every day and to consider whether they might be stabilising or even improving, and to adjust treatment accordingly (Appendix 3, 1.15-1.16). This did not appear to have happened in David's case.

7. The response of the consultant to the family's entirely reasonable request for nutrition and hydration to be continued to relieve the distress of hunger and dehydration, was in my experience, typical of malpractice under the LCP until it was stopped in 2014, but is unforgiveable in 2021. His refusal to place either a nasogastric tube or intravenous or subcutaneous cannula to offer the small amounts of daily fluids that are known in many cases to give comfort with minimal side-effects, disregards the guidance of the GMC (2010, Appendix 4) and of NICE guidance (2015) (NG31, Appendix 3, section 1.4).

From the evidence I have seen that David continued to live for several days in this state of withdrawn medication and withheld comfort fluids, in my opinion this would amount to a breach of duty of care leading to an accelerated death. It does not matter clinically if the person had advanced heart failure and would die eventually anyway. We know that it is very difficult to predict the timing of death in such patients, many of whom – as David himself had done just weeks before – can make temporary improvements.

To inflict extra suffering by holding back conventional treatments that could relieve breathlessness and the distress caused by increasing heart failure, and withholding fluids that could palliate the pangs of dehydration and starvation – especially for a person who was often being lucid and able to converse – could be seen as inflicting a cruel death sentence.

It was four days after treatment was withdrawn and fluids being withheld, that a swallowing assessment was performed. It should be clear to any layperson that this should have been performed on the first day of his going onto an "end of life" pathway. The fact that the assessment showed that he was still capable of swallowing safely, is a damning indictment of the poor judgement and cruel action of the clinical team.

8. I was shocked to read of the incident when David was aware and able to express his wish for treatment and hence continuing to live, and the family were forcibly stopped in recording this discussion. If the hospital security staff did indeed confiscate the family's phone, I would think this could be grounds for a legal action against the trust or security firm.

9. In conclusion, the withdrawal of cardiac failure treatment could have only one result and that is the rapid acceleration of cardiac failure. We are told that even the initiation of a syringe driver, presumably to offer mitigation of the effects of withdrawal and palliation of pain, breathlessness and distress, failed to achieve those humane intentions. This suggests to me that the cardiology team, on top of their poor clinical judgement and what appears to be negligent practice, also failed to call in palliative care specialists in David's care, as recommended explicitly for such situations by NICE guideline NG31:

"1.5.8 Regularly reassess, at least daily, the dying person's symptoms during treatment to inform appropriate titration[1] of medicine.

Seek specialist palliative care advice if the dying person's symptoms do not improve promptly with treatment or if there are undesirable side effects, such as unwanted sedation."

Coupled with the persistent use of the LCP-like blanket approach, the withholding of fluids, and this apparent lack of palliative care consultation together represent in my view a most serious breach of duty of care which could have contributed to an untimely and distressing death for David. If these observations are verified, then I am advised there is a possibility of bringing proceedings for an alleged personal or corporate act (or both) of homicide.

---

[1] 'Titration' here means the daily adjustment of doses of symptom-relieving drugs – both up or down, depending on the patient's response. It may also include switching to another drug if the first one fails to achieve its purpose, e.g. pain control.

Legal Overview

James Bogle, barrister

The case studies set out in this report make harrowing reading. What is of particular concern and is highlighted by Professor Sam Ahmedzai in both his introduction and his comments on the case studies, is the extent to which a succession of mistakes and clinical errors, frequently coupled with a lack of proper communication with, or even concern for, the patient and his or her family, occurs.

Moreover, these are but representative cases, reported with the permission of the families concerned, reflective of what we believe are many other such cases occurring in our health service which, in turn, represent a significant level of failure across the whole NHS.

Indeed, the report[1] ("the Neuberger report") of the independent review panel, set up in 2013 by Mr Norman Lamb MP, then Minister of State for Community and Social Care, and chaired by Baroness Neuberger, to review the rapidly expanding use of the Liverpool Care Pathway (LCP), after reviewing some 650 submissions, arrived at some disturbing findings regarding the state of end of life care in our health service.

How has this state of affairs come about in our health service and how has it been allowed to continue for so long without proper investigation or regulation?

I am a practising barrister who has spent part of some 30 years practice involved in end of life legal cases, some of which have ended in court and some not, some are reported cases and some not. I have also been involved in numerous clinical negligence and fatal accident cases. During that time, I have seen many developments in the care of patients at the end of their lives which involve trends that are often sub-optimal and sometimes disturbing.

The view expressed in this Legal Overview are mine and not necessarily those of the other contributors or publishers.

These trends have developed over a lengthy period of time and have arisen gradually so that the public, and even MPs and ministers, have not always fully appreciated or understood their significance and, for the most part, may not be aware of the failures.

The Neuberger report found that the relatively untested LCP had begun to decline into a blanket or box-ticking exercise in too many cases. Instead of being a tool or aid to clinical decision-making it had started to become a substitute for thinking. Once on the pathway, it was difficult for a patient to be taken off it and it was all too readily assumed that, if a patient was on the LCP, then he or she would inevitably die even when the patient may have had the capacity to survive and even thrive.

Case Study 1 is an example of this and, regrettably, it is not atypical.

The cases during the period of the LCP

Case Study 1

The patient was placed on the LCP, was put on a syringe driver sedating him with a mix of midazolam and morphine, ostensibly to ease pain. A junior doctor, of 4 months experience, acting alone and on night shift, made the decision. The patient then, it seems, died from the sedation and not from his clinical condition.

It is not uncommon for patients, thought to be terminal, to be placed on a syringe driver in that way, for the dosage to be increased to "make the patient comfortable" (sometimes even when the patient is not actually suffering any pain), and, when the patient dies, a doubt remains as to whether the patient died from his or her condition or from incremental doses of the potentially lethal combination of midazolam and morphine.

There were even cases of misdiagnosis where a patient had been declared to have a terminal condition (often cancer), was placed on the pathway and died but, after post-mortem, and to the quite unimaginable distress of the families, was found not to have had the diagnosed terminal disease at all.[2]

It remains a criminal homicide to bring about a patient's death deliberately, recklessly or negligently, although under the principle of "double effect" or "dual effect", one may administer drugs to relieve the pain even if life is unintentionally shortened.

However, the conclusions of some clinical trials and studies[3] has been that, in fact, the provision of pain relief and palliative care can tend to lengthen, not shorten, life, seemingly on the basis that the patient's body is relieved from expending additional energy and resources on dealing with pain.

In Case Study 1, if the certification of the cause of death, stated on the death certificate, was, in effect, "the LCP", that was clearly improper. The LCP was a clinical protocol or pathway not a recognised clinical condition.

The experiences of Mrs Charlesworth-Smith with agencies such as the CQC, NHS England and others, has not been encouraging and appears to reveal a level of non-engagement with the public, and even complacency, by some agencies, as regards the current state of end of life care, which cannot be regarded as acceptable.

It was to be expected that, following the Neuberger report, closer scrutiny of end of life care, and associated protocols and pathways, would follow. However, such scrutiny still leaves much to be desired.

Case Study 2

Case Study 2 also occurred before the LCP was finally abandoned. The hospital took the case to the Court of Protection[4] and it subsequently became a landmark Supreme Court case[5] in which Lady Hale, senior presiding judge of the Supreme Court, gave the court's principal judgment and set out what the approach should be to the making of decisions about whether to give life-sustaining treatment in the case of persons lacking the capacity to make decisions for themselves.

Mr James' widow appealed against a decision of the Court of Appeal that it was in his best interests to have life-sustaining treatment withheld. Mr James had been placed on a ventilator in the critical care unit of a hospital operated by the respondent NHS trust. He was seriously ill and his prospects of leaving the critical care unit were low. Following a marked deterioration in his neurological state, he was considered to lack the capacity to make decisions about his medical treatment. The trust issued proceedings, seeking, among other things, a declaration that it would be in his best interests for certain treatments to be withheld "in the event of a clinical deterioration".

The judge concluded that it would not be appropriate to make the declaration, not being persuaded that, for the purposes of the Code of Practice under the Mental Capacity Act 2005, treatment would be futile or overly burdensome or that there was no prospect of recovery.

The patient's condition worsened by the time of the hearing of the trust's appeal in the Court of Appeal. The result was a reversal of decision, and the court made a declaration in similar terms to that sought by the trust. The patient died shortly thereafter. The patient's family had taken a different view from that of the trust: they thought that he had a discernible quality of life from which he gained pleasure and that he would want treatment up to the point where it became hopeless.

The Supreme Court dismissed the family's appeal. It held, in considering the best interests of this particular patient, at this particular time, and taking into account his welfare in the widest sense, including social and psychological, that treatment could now be withdrawn.

This, in effect, meant that clinicians were empowered to make decisions that were not purely clinical but also social, a move seen by some as a move toward legitimising doctors to make "quality of life" decisions that ought, rather, to be made by the patient or his family, not the State or the medical profession.

However, Lady Hale made it clear[6] that the starting point is a strong presumption in favour of staying alive and a profound respect for the sanctity of human life (reprising Lord Bingham in the case of *Airedale NHS Trust v Bland*[7]) and that, in considering the best interests of this particular patient, at this particular time, decision-makers must look at:

- his welfare in the widest sense;

- the prospects of success of the medical treatment;

- the likely outcome of that treatment for the patient;

- the likely attitude of the patient to the treatment; and

- what others who are looking after him, or are interested in his welfare, say about his likely attitude to the treatment.

Thus, although admitted for what was diagnosed as no more than constipation, the patient acquired an infection, pneumonia and sepsis, all conditions that tend to suggest poor care and treatment. The hospital, instead of treating the conditions, made a prognosis of septic shock, dehydration and organ failure, again all of which were eminently treatable, particularly dehydration, and claimed that treatment would be futile. They then sought withdrawal of all treatment with the intention that the patient would die.

In fact, the patient lived a further 7 months at the Critical Care Unit (CCU) which is an extraordinarily long time to be kept in the CCU, particularly as the patient was responding to treatments and progressing to the point of him being readied to return home. However, he caught yet further hospital-borne infections which led to his treatment being withdrawn.

Put shortly, the patient, of no great age, came into hospital with constipation but left hospital dead. There has been very little explanation by the court, the hospital, the NHS, the Ombudsman, the CQC, or FOI or subject access requests, as to how this was allowed to occur and why it was not avoided or, after the event, properly investigated. This is all clearly highly unsatisfactory, to say the very least.

The cases post-LCP

The first two deaths occurred while the Liverpool Care Pathway (LCP) was still in use; the next three occurred before the publication of NICE guideline NG31[8] and the last eleven deaths occurred after the publication of NG31. Instead of demonstrating an overall improvement in end of life care thereafter, they seem to indicate that similar disturbing problems are continuing to occur, and the pattern adopted under the LCP too often continues.

Case Study 3

Case Study 3 is a very disturbing case and there were multiple failures at many levels, some apparently more than merely negligent.

First, the patient had apparently been allowed to deteriorate over months at home without appropriate specialist cardiac and respiratory care which suggests a negligent breach of duty on the part of the three GPs who declined the family's pleas for referral. The family's request for a respiratory physiotherapist being also declined, this too suggests a negligent breach of duty.

Second, the patient may have been discharged from hospital too soon on 4 January 2014. This again suggests a negligent breach of duty. Third, the combination of failures resulting in his severe deterioration by 7 January 2014, suggests negligence at best. Fourth, the failure to call for an ambulance in a timely fashion suggests negligence, if not recklessness, resulting in respiratory failure.

Third, after the paramedics had apparently told the family that the patient was "okay" with independent respiratory and cardiac output, the claim by a consultant that he should be allowed to die was obtuse at best and suggested poor communication skills, poor diagnosis, negligent breach of duty if not recklessness. This was exacerbated by what followed thereafter.

Fourth, there followed a succession of events involving a nurse who purportedly had no name badge (itself questionable) fitting a tube nasally without any explanation to the patient or family, ignoring the greeting of the latter, another person, again with no name badge, giving the patient an injection without consulting him or the family or telling either why she was doing so and then walking out of the room whereupon the patient then died. This behaviour and action seem to obviously invite comment. There followed a callously indifferent request, made to the family without preparatory comment, by another person with no name badge, for permission for tissue removal of the now deceased patient.

This failure to follow even the most elementary of nurse-patient-family protocols and guidance adds yet further to the already high level of suspicion surrounding the whole incident. The insouciant and careless call down the corridor by another nurse to the family that a police officer was on the way to identify the body added further to the highly unsatisfactory nature of the interactions.

Fifth, there was no inquest and, so it seems, no referral to the coroner by clinical staff, despite the suspicious nature of the circumstances which, without more, ought to have led to such a referral. It is not clear what was written on the death certificate by the GP but that may have led to further suspicions.

Sixth, it later transpired that the patient had been given midazolam and morphine, a cocktail which has been observed to have the capacity to shorten life, despite the fact that he had not been in pain. That, too, suggests a negligent breach of duty at best, if not more. Even more disturbing is the fact that five doses of three other drugs were documented with exact times, but not the giving of morphine and midazolam. The inference arises that, within the team, there was likely a realisation that the co-administration of these drugs was directly responsible for the cessation of breathing.

Morphine was, in any case, redundant, the patient not being in pain, yet morphine, being an opiate analgesic, is a very powerful respiratory depressant and thus, in a patient already known to be in respiratory failure, on the face of matters, seemingly contra-indicated.

Seventh, despite the coroner's office apparently suggesting that the death was not due to natural causes, no inquest was arranged, again suggesting a negligent breach of duty. The task of the coroner, and of the clinicians who should report to him, and of the police, is not obviated by there being no early complaint by the family.

Eighth, despite the police apparently saying they were "looking at" a case of involuntary manslaughter, no proper investigation appears to have been undertaken, suggesting a failure by the police to carry out their duty to investigate a homicide. Their claim that the investigation had to be closed because there was no histology is clearly unsustainable and adds to the seriousness of the failure.

Ninth, the body appears to have been cremated prematurely and it is not clear if this was a decision of the family or some other agency. An intention to impede a proper enquiry could amount to a number of offences including obstructing both police enquiries (e.g. under s.89(2) of the Police Act 1996) and coronial enquiries (the common law offence of disposing of a body before the coroner can openly enquire) and possibly more. These are potentially serious offences.

Tenth, the person administering the apparently lethal injection was, it has been suggested, not registered on the GMC database as being a qualified clinician. If he were, in fact, unqualified, that would be a matter of considerable gravity involving a number of offences (e.g. under s.23 of the Offences Against the Person Act 1861 or s.49(1) of the Medical Act 1983). However, it seems unlikely that the trust or staff would allow such a major infringement of the law and there could be a number of explanations for this apparent discrepancy.

Eleventh, a falsified "Do Not Attempt to Resuscitate" (DNAR) order is said (by the family) to have been fabricated by a person claiming to be a doctor (and whom the family had never met) who claimed that the consent of the family had been obtained not to resuscitate the patient. That, if true, would be particularly disturbing. Fabrication, again, seems unlikely but certainly merited further investigation.

It is an offence to falsify or fabricate a medical record or document (including under s.33(1) of the Health and Safety at Work Act 1974, possibly also the Forgery and Counterfeiting Act 1981 and the Fraud Act 2006, among other provisions).

Further, since the Francis Inquiry into the Mid-Staffordshire NHS Foundation Trust, it is also an offence, under s.92 of the Care Act 2014, for certain care providers to supply false information. That Cheshire CID accepted this document at face value is also concerning and suggests a further breach of duty.

Finally, the fact that there was never a terminal diagnosis at any stage makes the various failures, breaches and offences all the more disturbing.

It is suggested that an inquest jury might have brought in a verdict of unlawful homicide and, if the facts are as stated above, that seems possible. Indeed, if the facts are all as stated, a case for alleged involuntary manslaughter by the perpetrators concerned, may have been made out. Moreover, there being no limitation period for such serious offences, such a prosecution could, in theory, still be brought although, given the lack of police interest at the time, it would be harder to persuade police to investigate now, many years later. That, of course, makes this remarkably distressing and disturbing case all the more so.

However, bringing such legal claims requires initiative, focus, stamina, sufficient funds, good lawyers and a determination which is often lacking in the recently bereaved. This is the case with all of the case studies herein and is usually a major hurdle to the families of victims taking any legal action.

Case Study 4

In 2015, the patient, aged 86, with diabetes, was admitted to hospital with pneumonia (having previously had a pleural effusion, now recurring) and a probable underlying respiratory condition (e.g. chronic bronchitis or obstructive pulmonary disease) and a serious form of lung failure. The patient could talk, eat and drink but was bed-bound after a leg break and she needed hoisting. She was given an estimated discharge date and not considered to be dying. Her effusion was drained of 1.5 litres of fluid.

However, from being written down as swallowing normally with no issues present, she was soon, and seemingly abruptly, designated "nil by mouth" (NBM), even though no swallow test had been undertaken. Then her daily medicines were stopped even including her heart medication, Bisoprolol.

Once again, the familiar pattern of poor communication by clinical staff with the family is seen and this seems to have been a prominent problem in this case. The family, being unaware that she was designated NBM, fed her solid food which she not only wanted (having had nothing for a whole week) but which she swallowed with no difficulty at all.

The family say that a medical registrar, having commented that it was "not a nice life to be hoisted" then placed the patient on an end of life pathway. Despite having an intravenous (IV) drip, the patient was shown by blood tests to be dehydrated but, instead of increasing fluid, it was decreased and a pressurised oxygen mask fitted (Bi-level Positive Airways Pressure or BiPAP) for Type 2 respiratory failure.

She was then diagnosed as "dying", apparently with no fluids at all given for 24 hours and, so the family state, the consultant, when asked to re-fit the patient's drip, refused to do so, virtually guaranteeing death thereby from dehydration, a very unpleasant way to die. The patient's oedema was apparently also left untreated. Unsurprisingly, the patient died not long after the removal of the drip.

As with Case Study 2, this appears to have been another alleged case of an avoidable death occasioned by neglect if not more, exacerbated by poor communication. Allowing death by neglect of a person in one's care, and to whom one owes a duty of care, is potentially a homicide.[9] The NICE guideline NG31, published at the end of 2015, appears not to have been properly followed. In 2017, the Health Ombudsman partially upheld a family complaint against the trust.

The conclusion of Professor Patrick Pullicino, the neurologist referred to by the Kent Police Serious Case Review, is particularly troubling:
"… prolonged dehydration would certainly have contributed to her death and given that she had no fluids at all for the last 48 hours of her life, it could even have been the principal cause of death."

Revealingly, responding to a complaint from the family in June 2016, the chief executive of the hospital trust was, in effect, obliged to admit a series of failures, particularly of lack of communication with the family.

The failures did not end there. Additionally, Kent Police initiated a serious case review but appear to have failed to act on the findings of expert witness, Professor Pullicino. The case was not referred to the coroner and yet this case clearly called for such a report. Given the comments of Professor Pullicino, consultant neurologist, the Ombudsman's findings and the hospital's admission of mistakes, the GMC's apparent failure to find evidence of poor practice by doctors seems difficult to explain. The lack of adequate response from the CQC also seems highly unsatisfactory.

This, then, is another case where proceedings for alleged involuntary manslaughter against hospital and staff may have been indicated. In addition, no person, including patients, may be subject to torture or degrading and inhuman treatment, since such is contrary to their human rights under Article 3 of the European Convention and the Human Rights Act 1998 ("the Convention").

To dehydrate a patient to death is an extremely painful and distressing way to die and is not always relieved by mere analgesic pain relief. Accordingly, unless the clinical staff can be sure that the patient is not suffering such distress, they must not allow dehydration lest the patient's Article 3 rights are thereby violated.

However, as mentioned above, bringing such legal claims requires sufficient funds and a determination which is often lacking in the recently bereaved. This is the case with all the case studies herein and is usually a hurdle to the families of victims taking any legal action.

Case Study 5

The patient was admitted to hospital as an emergency following a fall at home but, on the basis that clinical staff considered that she apparently had but a single fractured eighth rib on the right side, she was considered suitable for discharge the following day. She was discharged, after only one day, with no pain medication or care package and the Ombudsman found this to be a failure. This again appears to be a negligent breach of duty. She was re-admitted, 2 days later, with haemothorax requiring a drain of blood. She died 3 weeks later, still in hospital.

Although an inquest found this to be an "accidental death", her daughter pursued the matter further and uncovered further issues: during the second admission, she was found to have multiple rib fractures of the right chest; on 26 September 2015, she had accidentally imbibed some of an open bottle of anti-bacterial agent, left by her bed, which later correspondence reveals caused her final deterioration, and this appears to be a negligent breach of duty that contributed to her death. There appears to be no evidence that she was admitted with pneumonia or pneumothorax. Multiple rib fractures were later seen on a CT scan after the second admission date, but the Ombudsman seems to be suggesting that they may have occurred after the first fall and that they were missed by clinical staff.

Concerns raised about the withdrawal of her medications and of oral fluids were, it seems, largely ignored and the patient was hastily placed on an "end of life care" pathway which, the daughter says, closely resembled the LCP (even though the LCP was no longer in use). Diamorphine was prescribed even though, it seems, it was contra-indicated and may even have added to her "breakthrough" pain. If so, that seems also to be a negligent breach of duty. No subcutaneous fluids were given, only swabs, and she appears to have suffered dehydration. This, too, appears negligent.

Notwithstanding the finding at inquest, this death appears to have been preventable and may have been caused by a negligent breach of duty. If so, then, once again, proceedings for an alleged homicide may have been indicated. Once again, the matter was left entirely to the bereaved family rather than the responsible agents of the State taking proper steps to protect life. The patient may also have had a claim (via her estate) for personal injury, having been caused pain, suffering and loss of amenity by any alleged negligent breach of duty. However, fatal accident claims are governed by old and out-dated law, less and less suited to modern clinical conditions and providing limited redress.[10]

Complaints to the GMC about end of life care are not often successful so that, increasingly, the course now most likely to impact upon negligent care of the elderly in our hospitals is to bring proceedings for alleged culpable homicide.

In the 1992 case of Dr Nigel Cox,[11] despite his being convicted of attempted murder, the professional conduct committee of the GMC decided to take no further action beyond reprimand. Cox returned to his former job in February 1993, albeit under supervision.

Case Study 6

This patient had cancer and was refused hydration in her last week of life.

Professor Ahmedzai's opinion is that there was a clear breach of duty of care by the clinicians who denied the lady the comfort and dignity of having assisted fluids. He considers their justifications unsustainable given that, 18 months after the publication of NICE guideline NG31, they were not prepared to accept and implement its recommendations.

A claim in negligence can be defended if there is proof that a group of doctors, skilled in the area concerned, would have acted the same way, and provided they can explain logically the rationale for their decision.[12]

The Director of Nursing and Patient Services made an attempt to defend the trust but it is difficult to identify a clear and sustainable defence. Professor Ahmedzai states in his opinion that there appears to have been a clear negligent breach of duty by the clinicians who had denied the lady the comfort and dignity of having assisted fluids. The reasons they gave, including expense, lack of training and equipment do not appear material, because offering assisted hydration in different ways has been standard practice in hospitals, and indeed in hospices, for decades and the knowledge and equipment are readily available.

Professor Ahmedzai concludes that denying this patient a trial of assisted hydration could not have been logically supported by any group of medical peers at that time which appears to indicate that proceedings for alleged negligent breach of duty may have been indicated and, if this led to her death, could provide a potential basis for proceedings for alleged involuntary homicide.

Case Study 7

This was a particularly disturbing case. For a 21-year-old lady with severe learning disabilities to go into hospital for a "routine" eye operation, and to die three and a half weeks later without her nutritional needs having been met, such that a coroner found that malnutrition contributed significantly to her death, is particularly harrowing. This is all the more so, given that her parents were asking daily for assessments and clinical assistance with nutrition to be given.

This appears to be another case where proceedings for alleged homicide may have been indicated. In addition, there may have been cause to bring a case of alleged disability discrimination under the Equality Act

2010 and under Article 2 (right to life), Article 3 (freedom from degrading and inhuman treatment), Article 8 (right to private and family life) and Article 14 (freedom from discrimination) of the Convention.

In addition, given that the patient was also mentally incapacitated, Professor Ahmedzai draws attention to the hospital's apparent failure to call a "Best Interests" meeting as is usually required for persons lacking mental capacity. That alleged failure appears to be a breach of s.4(7) of the Mental Capacity Act 2005 and of Article 8 (right to private and family life) of the Convention.

Case Study 8

This patient was 86 years old, very fit and went into hospital for a routine knee operation. This was another distressing case of an apparent and alleged failure to provide proper nutrition and hydration so that the patient's daughter is fairly certain that her mother died of dehydration.

Again, there was an apparent and alleged failure to follow NICE guideline NG31, as well as GMC guidance 2010,[13] in the view of Professor Ahmedzai. Withholding (and indeed, actually withdrawing) clinically assisted hydration from a previously fit older person who came into hospital for an elective procedure, appears to represent a neglect contributing to her death. Proceedings for alleged negligent homicide may have been indicated.

There might also be subsidiary civil claims for alleged negligent breach of duty, including the loss of the hearing aids and the failure to replace them, and under Article 2 (right to life), Article 3 (freedom from degrading and inhuman treatment) and Article 8 (right to private and family life) of the Convention. There may have been scope for a secondary victim claim by her daughter given the alleged distress and psychiatric harm that she may have suffered from being unable to assist her mother in her latter days and hours, because of the badly managed end of life situation.

Case Study 9

In this case the patient had lung cancer that had spread to his brain, abdomen and other areas of his body, in spite of standard oncological care consisting of high dose palliative radiotherapy, followed by palliative chemotherapy and further radiotherapy to the brain. He was thought to have progressive disease and transfer was arranged to the local Marie Curie hospice. However, this again is another case where nutrition and hydration may have been neglected if not, indeed, actively withheld, and the relevant guidance not followed.

The case also demonstrates the inadequacy of the current complaint processes not only internal to the health service but externally. There is a preponderance of avenues of complaint, but they too frequently prove inadequate and more directed toward a cosmetic appearance of action but with little or no actual redress.

In the event, subcutaneous fluids were indeed started. However, from the wife's account it appears that this was "hit and miss" and she alleges that the patient actually received insufficient fluids in the time the infusion was running before he died.

Professor Ahmedzai comments that he was shocked to learn that, in a British hospice in 2017, the staff first prevaricated about placing a subcutaneous cannula and then did not perform the procedure correctly. He concludes that this appears to demonstrate a clear negligent breach of duty with respect to both the GMC guidance 2010 and NICE guideline NG31.

Extensive documentation supplied by the patient's widow shows that she also raised other concerns regarding the way that the DNACPR form was handled in the hospice. Later enquiry appears to have failed to take proper account of this. The wife also asked whether the patient had been placed on the LCP, or a variation of it, but seems to have been met with evasion.

Professor Ahmedzai's conclusion is that the hospice in question was still operating in a manner reproducing the kind of misuse of the LCP that occurred prior to the Neuberger report.

Proceedings for alleged homicide by neglect may again have been indicated, together with possible subsidiary civil claims for alleged negligent breach of duty and under Article 2 (right to life), Article 3 (freedom from degrading and inhuman treatment) and Article 8 (right to private and family life) of the Convention.

There might also be a secondary victim claim by the widow, given the alleged distress and psychiatric harm that she may have suffered from any effect upon her of a badly managed end of life situation.

Case Study 10

The first of these cases is again one where nutrition and hydration appear to have been withheld and guidance not followed.

In the absence of a court order to withhold all sustenance, to inflict death by enforcing malnutrition and dehydration remains a potential homicide. It is also a very unpleasant way for anyone to die and is just as unpleasant for the relatives and family, as the patient wastes away and dehydrates. Relatives have been heard to remark that they would not treat an animal in such a way.

The allegedly aggressive conduct of the doctor in insisting upon a DNACPR order also seems unacceptable. This is particularly so where agreeing to such an order is often interpreted by hospital staff as condoning withdrawal of other forms of life-sustaining, and even comfort, treatments.

The second case concerned her mother and again the same issues arose. She was allegedly treated inappropriately by purportedly being given no opportunity for assistance with drinking or of assisted hydration with a drip. This appears to have become a not entirely uncommon scenario in the health service and indeed one which was raised many times in the Neuberger report. It would have been unacceptable for a nursing home not to be equipped to offer clinically-assisted nutrition and hydration (CANH).

It would also have been unacceptable for decisions to be made behind the back of the daughter who held a welfare power of attorney under the Mental Capacity Act 2005. She was entitled to be consulted, and should have been consulted, about treatment decisions, if her mother lacked mental capacity which, given that she suffered from Alzheimer's, seems to have been the case at least some of the time.

S.4(7) of the Mental Capacity Act 2005 requires that decision-makers:

"must take into account, if it is practicable and appropriate to consult them, the views of...(c) any donee of a lasting power of attorney granted by [the patient]."

Failure to do so may violate the patient's rights under Article 8 (right to private and family life) of the Convention.[14]

Once again proceedings for alleged homicide by neglect may have been indicated, together with possible subsidiary civil claims for alleged negligent breach of duty and under Article 2 (right to life), Article 3 (freedom from degrading and inhuman treatment) and Article 8 (right to private and family life) of the Convention.

There might also be a potential secondary victim claim given the alleged distress and psychiatric harm that may have been suffered if the end of life care was badly managed.

Case Study 11

The patient was diagnosed with bowel cancer in 2015 but was not imminently dying and yet died in the hospice prematurely. This was another case where nutrition and hydration appear to have been withheld and guidance not followed. In this case the apparently condescending attitude of staff in allegedly attempting to pressure the wife into agreeing to withdraw or withhold hydration would have been unacceptable, if true.

The extreme reluctance of the wife to lodge a complaint or raise concerns is by no means untypical, because families are often traumatised by the experience of their loved one's end of life care. That is a particularly disturbing feature of many such cases and, when coupled with the complexity and often ineffectiveness of complaints procedures in achieving any real redress, this means that these serious cases can often escape proper and effective scrutiny so that they risk being repeated with impunity, time and again.

The GMC guidance 2010 recommends that the dying patient's wish for hydration (or of those close to the patient) "will usually be the deciding factor" and the hospice appears to have failed to follow the guidance. In the opinion of Professor Ahmedzai, the patient's death, while inevitable because of the advanced stage of his cancer, was possibly accelerated, and certainly made more unpleasant, by the reluctance to adhere promptly to this guidance.

Once again proceedings for alleged homicide by neglect may have been indicated, together with potential subsidiary civil claims for alleged negligent breach of duty and under Article 2 (right to life), Article 3 (freedom from degrading and inhuman treatment) and Article 8 (right to private and family life) of the Convention.

There might also be a potential secondary victim claim due to any alleged distress and psychiatric harm arising out of the effect of any badly managed end of life situation.

Case Study 12

This was a case of an elderly mother in pain with undiagnosed gastric (stomach) cancer not referred to an oncologist or specialist, and where there was no cohesive care or pain management.

It is another case where there appears to have been the uncritical application of a protocol, in similar fashion to that of the now abandoned LCP, contrary to the NICE guideline NG31 and the GMC guidance 2010.

In addition, in this case spanning nearly two years, a 94-year-old lady had abdominal symptoms that appear to have gone largely uninvestigated so that, finally, when a diagnosis of gastric cancer was made, it was allegedly too late to treat other than palliatively. An allegation of negligent breach of duty may have been indicated.

Any poor communication allegedly shown by the clinical and nursing staff would have added to the potential negligence and, even if insufficient to give rise to a secondary claim by the patient's son, would require investigation and, if demonstrated, remedy.

Poor communication may indicate a lack of transparency over certain end of life decisions which can, in turn, conceal problems and possible negligence, and, equally importantly, cause considerable and unnecessary distress and alarm to relatives and family, particularly where they are simply told that the patient is dying (or even dead) without any preamble. That is inevitably bound to cause the most acute distress in any of a patient's relatives. Such a lack of transparency would be contrary to the NICE guideline NG31 and the GMC guidance 2010. If this culture is still continuing in the health service then it needs urgent attention.

The response of the coroner's office, and the apparent refusal of the pathologist to check blood levels, would, if demonstrated, have had the effect of tending to conceal any potential negligent breach of duty that may have occurred and would tend to undermine the very point and purpose of a coronial enquiry.

Even if there had been a negligent breach of duty leading to death that might give rise to a fatal accident claim but, as mentioned elsewhere, the law relating to fatal accident claims is now arguably quite out of date and may not achieve a satisfactory remedy. On the other hand, if it could be shown that death had been caused by any negligence or recklessness then, once again, criminal proceedings for alleged involuntary homicide might be indicated.

Case Study 13

This patient had been diagnosed with dementia but seems to have been treated inappropriately from the outset. In addition to dehydration, this was an occasion where prescription of fludrocortisone and lorazepam, seemingly without a clear reason (at least not known to his next of kin, or which later became evident to Professor Ahmedzai) and without evidence of regular blood monitoring for low potassium, may have caused or contributed to death. If so, proceedings for an alleged homicide may thereby be indicated.

In addition, the patient appears to have been placed unilaterally on a Deprivation of Liberty safeguard (DOLS),[15] seemingly without the family's knowledge, which is potentially unlawful as the DOLS procedure required consultation with the family. Moreover, it is alleged that a DNACPR was signed without consulting the relative who held an LPA. If so, that might have been a breach of s.4(7) of the Mental Capacity Act 2005 and a violation of the patient's Article 8 (right to private and family life) rights.[16] Simply put, if the daughter could show that the DOLS procedure had not been followed that might have been unlawful and an order might have been obtainable against the hospital, with damages and costs. Unlawful deprivation of liberty is a violation of a person's rights under Article 5 (right to liberty and security) and possibly Article 8 (right to private and family life) of the Convention.

In *Re: SR,*[17] it was held unjustifiable to prevent a husband taking his wife out of a care home in which she resided. In *Hillingdon LBC v Neary*[18] the Court found a local authority had acted unlawfully in failing to follow DOLS safeguards and failing to respect the patient's rights under Article 5 (right to liberty) and Article 8 (right to private and family life) of the Convention. In *G v E (Costs)* [2011] EWCA Civ 939, the Court awarded costs against a local authority that had acted in breach of the DOLS requirements.

However, if there is poor communication and a consequent lack of transparency, abuses and breaches can often go unnoticed giving rise to yet more distress, difficulty and poor end of life care.

Case Study 14

This patient had Type 1 diabetes and end-stage renal failure. The case seems to be another example of poor communication, contrary to NICE guideline NG31, recommendation 1.2, and the GMC guidance 2010 leading, again, to a lack of transparency which, in turn, may hide other failings.

It seems clear from the daughter's account that the hospital may have been aware from Christmas Eve, if not Christmas Day itself, that the father was deteriorating rapidly and in an unexplained and thus unpredictable way. It appears that the hospital concluded, at around this time, that the patient had lost mental capacity. If so, this ought to have led to the family being called in for a discussion about medical decision-making and the patient's preferences, pursuant to s.4(7) of the Mental Capacity Act 2005. The clinical staff's alleged failure to attempt to engage the family in "best interests" discussions and decision-making would, if demonstrated, have been a breach of the patient's human rights, particularly Article 8 (right to private and family life).

Second, if there is any suspicion of an unexplained death, it is the duty of attending clinicians to notify the coroner's office. If this was not done, it would have been a breach of the Notification of Deaths Regulations 2019, a reportable professional offence.

Finally, the DNACPR decision, allegedly made without consulting the relatives (one of whom may have had an LPA) may have led to the patient's death which, again, might have been a breach of his Article 8 (right to private and family life) rights,[19] and, if it did lead to the patient's death, might indicate scope for proceedings for a fatal accident and/or alleged homicide.

Case Study 15

This patient was diagnosed with small cell lung cancer in December 2019, which had metastasized to her brain by January 2021. This was another case that seemed to show hallmarks of the old, abandoned, LCP with its tendency to a "tick-box" and "one size fits all" approach that led to complaints about its use as an end of life protocol. Denying hydration again has the hallmark of the old, abandoned LCP practices.

In addition, the hospice community team's apparent failure to keep written care plans appears to have been in breach of the NICE guideline

NG31 and of associated quality standards (e.g. QS144, 2017[20]). The patient may also have been over-sedated. Sedation could have been lessened in order to allow her to communicate with her family.

The hospice would need to show that they had individualised care plans in place (whether written or not) and that they were following these. These should normally be included in records of communication with the patient and family.

Professor Ahmedzai cites part of QS144 to the effect that adults in the last days of life, and the people important to them, must be given opportunities to discuss, develop and review an individualised care plan.

In his opinion, the alleged failure of St Luke's Hospice team to have such a procedure seems to represent a breach of their duty of care, for which the hospice management might even be held corporately responsible.

This, if demonstrated, might also be a breach of the patients' Article 8 (right to private and family life) rights. Further, if the denial of hydration and nutrition caused or contributed to the patient's death, then proceedings for alleged involuntary homicide might have been indicated.

Case Study 16

This case is another deeply distressing and harrowing one. It was also another case that seemed to show the attributes of the old, abandoned, LCP "template" being imposed uncritically and negligently. It appears to have caused the patient to have a painful and desperate end and that, unsurprisingly, appears to have considerably traumatised his relatives.

The patient appears to have been wrongly denied cardiac follow-ups and then to have been diagnosed as "terminal" and placed on a seemingly inappropriate "pathway". There would have been, if demonstrated, poor communication with the family creating a feeling of lack of transparency over clinical decisions. Using the COVID pandemic as a reason for unilaterally withdrawing the patient's cardiac treatment, if demonstrated, would also appear to give rise to an allegation of negligent breach of duty.

The refusal to place either a nasogastric tube or intravenous or subcutaneous cannula to offer small amounts of daily fluids to give comfort, with minimal side-effects, would appear, if demonstrated, to disregard the

GMC guidance 2010 and NICE guideline NG31, section 1.4 and, if demonstrated, might also appear to give rise to an allegation of negligent breach of duty, if not more.

That the patient died as a result, may, if causation and a direct connection were demonstrated, also provide scope for possible proceedings for alleged homicide, his heart condition notwithstanding. The fact that a swallowing assessment showed that the patient was still able to swallow safely seems particularly egregious. The alleged confiscation of the family's mobile phone to prevent a report is also disturbing and, if demonstrated, gives rise to further concern, particularly given that the family apparently desired only to record the patient's wish for treatment and hydration.

It is also suggested that the cardiology team allegedly failed to call in palliative specialists, contrary to the NICE guideline NG31, and so it is further alleged that they failed to care for the patient appropriately.

Professor Ahmedzai states his opinion that the withholding of fluids, the apparent lack of palliative care consultation, coupled with the old LCP "blanket" approach, appears to represent, in his view, a personal or corporate act (or both) of negligence leading to death and thus scope for possible proceedings for alleged homicide.

The further difficulty, as ever, was the isolation suffered by bereaved relatives, trying to cope with their grief, whilst feeling that they had been failed by the very institutions that should have been protecting them and their loved ones from harm.

In such circumstances, it is unsurprising that grieving relatives do not often contemplate the commencement of proceedings. They naturally feel that they ought to be able to rely upon the relevant agencies to protect the rights of their loved ones.

That, it may be argued, is why few such criminal proceedings have thus far been brought in such cases.

Conclusion

This report has cited 16 examples, in the words of the families concerned, of some particularly harrowing and disturbing cases which the public have a right to expect could and should never have arisen. Moreover, it seems that the whole burden for seeking accountability has too often been largely laid upon the shoulders of the bereaved themselves who, unsurprisingly, are too distressed to be able to take much action beyond coping with their grief.

To say that such a situation is unsatisfactory is to say the very least. To add to the burden of already suffering and bereaved relatives is contrary to what our care quality standards and human rights ought to entail and are meant to encompass. As noted above, bringing complaints, and especially legal claims, requires sufficient funds and a determination which is often lacking in the recently bereaved and, as with all of the case studies herein, is usually a major hurdle to the families of victims taking any legal action.

The obvious place to debate the matter is Parliament, although the debate, of course, needs to be held on a wider scale. Accordingly, our "Call for Remedial Actions" chapter seeks to suggest solutions and remedies and will ask Parliamentarians to address current shortcomings, as a matter of urgency.

It is in the interests of all, whether patients, families or clinicians, that dying patients be afforded better end of life care and that their bereaved families be treated with care and respect. Families should be aided, and not burdened, when faced with the distress of seeing their loved ones suffering and should have speedier, effective and more satisfactory resolutions of their complaints when anything goes wrong.

In a modern health service such as ours this ought to be routine and normal.

Addendum – certification of death

In the well-known 1957 case of Dr Bodkin-Adams,[21] and, more recently, in the 1992 case of Dr Cox,[22] the defendants claimed that their intention was not to shorten life but to relieve pain and that thus, on the principle of double effect, they should be acquitted of homicide. Adams was believed and acquitted, Cox was not.

However, public opinion was greatly aroused by the case of Dr Harold Shipman[23] in which the defendant did not even pretend that he was only relieving pain. Moreover, there were not merely one or two patients involved but some 250.

In 2003, the Shipman Inquiry, chaired by Dame Janet Smith, proposed that there should be an effective cross-check of the account of events given by the doctor who treated the deceased and who claimed to be able to identify the cause of death, regardless of whether the death was followed by burial or cremation.

In response, after a long period of policy development, a system of medical examiners was introduced by Parliament in the Coroners and Justice Act 2009. Concerns, however, have continued and the Health and Care Act 2022 was introduced in the House of Commons on 6 July 2021 and received royal assent on 28 April 2022, making further amendments regarding medical examiners.

The system of death certification in England and Wales requires certification of the cause of death by a registered medical practitioner, "to the best of their knowledge and belief", pursuant to s.22 of the Births and Deaths Registration Act 1953. Alternatively, the death must have been reported to the coroner and the appropriate certificate provided by them.

Of the offences set out under the 1953 Act, there are none relating to a doctor stating falsely the cause of death on a certificate. The assumption seems to have been that doctors would not do so. However, under s.4 of the Perjury Act 1911 (still good law) it is an offence to falsify a death certificate.[24] We may take it this applies equally to doctors who so falsify.

The Office for National Statistics guidance on death certification (updated 25 March 2022)[25] reminds clinicians that:

"...prompt and accurate certification of death is essential as it serves a number of functions. A medical certificate of cause of death (MCCD) enables the deceased's family to register the death. This provides a permanent legal record of the fact of death and enables the family to arrange disposal of the body, and to settle the deceased's estate."

The guidance further requires that deaths be registered within 5 days of their occurrence unless there is to be a coroner's post-mortem or an inquest. The next of kin gets a certified copy of the register entry ("death certificate") with an exact copy of the cause of death which must include "clear, accurate and complete information in a timely manner about the diseases or conditions" that caused the death.

Failing this, the death must be referred to the coroner. Doctors (under the Notification of Deaths Regulations 2019[26]) and registrars of births and deaths (under the Registration of Births and Deaths Regulations 1987[27]) have a legal obligation to report certain categories of deaths to the coroner before they can be registered.

These include deaths where there is reason to suspect the death was unnatural, unknown, violent or where the death occurs in custody or otherwise in State detention. This can include where the death is due to the person undergoing a treatment or procedure of a medical or similar nature: for example, a death during an operation or before full recovery from an anaesthetic.

Following the 2003 Shipman Inquiry, the Coroners and Justice Act 2009 provided for a system of death certification under which all deaths in England and Wales that do not require investigation by a coroner will be subject to scrutiny by independent medical examiners. The statutory scheme (as amended) provides for local authorities in England, and Local Health Boards in Wales, to appoint medical examiners to provide greater scrutiny of deaths. Given the length of time since the Shipman Inquiry recommendations, this is long overdue.

According to a House of Commons library research briefing dated 3 November 2021, the legislative provisions are not yet fully implemented. However, the system will be run within the NHS and is being rolled out.[28]

The stated purpose of the medical examiner system is to:

- provide greater safeguards for the public by ensuring proper scrutiny of all non-coronial deaths

- ensure the appropriate direction of deaths to the coroner

- provide a better service for the bereaved and an opportunity for them to raise any concerns to a doctor not involved in the care of the deceased

- improve the quality of death certification

- improve the quality of mortality data.

The purpose of medical examiners is to avoid any recurrence of misuse of death certification as in the Shipman case.

1 *More Care, Less Pathway: a review of the Liverpool Care Pathway*, Report of the Independent Review of the Liverpool Care Pathway, Department of Health and Social Care, 15 July 2013.

2 See, for example, CMAJ. 2010 Jan 12; 182(1): 17-18 at https://www.ncbi.nlm.nih.gov/pmc/articles/ PMC2802600/ where the patient, Mr Jones, died needlessly having beaten his cancer but was not taken off the pathway, not treated for a chest infection and so died. Thereafter, it was found that he had no cancer and, with treatment, could have survived.

3 See, for example, this study in *The New England Journal of Medicine*: Temel MD, J T *et al*, "Early Palliative Care for Patients with Metastatic Non–Small-Cell Lung Cancer", N Engl J Med 2010; 363:733-742, reported in *The New York Times* here: https://www.nytimes.com/2010/08/19/health/19care.html .

4 The Court of Protection used to be an office of the Senior Courts but, with the advent of the Mental Capacity Act 2005 it has become a full-fledged court of record handling cases involving those lacking mental capacity.

5 *Aintree University Hospitals NHS Foundation Trust v James* [2013] UKSC 67, [2014] AC 591, [2013] 10 WLUK 970.

6 [2013] UKSC 67, para 39.

7 [1993] AC 789, [1993] 2 WLUK 69.

8 *Care of dying adults in the last days of life*, guideline NG31, National Institute for Health and Care Excellence, 16 December 2015.

9 *R v Gibbins and Proctor* (1919) 13 Cr App R 134.

10 See the Law Reform (Miscellaneous Provisions) Act 1934 and the Fatal Accidents Act 1976.

11 *R v Cox* [1992] 12 BMLR 38.

12 *Bolitho v City and Hackney Health Authority* [1998] A.C. 232, [1997] 3 W.L.R. 1151, [1997] 4 All E.R. 771; *Bolam v Friern Hospital Management Committee* [1957] 1 W.L.R. 582, [1957] 2 All E.R. 118.

13 *Treatment and care towards the end of life: good practice in decision making.* General Medical Council. Published 20 May 2010 and updated 15 March 2022.

14 *Winspear v City Hospitals Sunderland NHS Foundation Trust* [2015] EWHC 3250 (QB), [2016] Q.B. 691, [2016] 2 W.L.R. 1089, following in *R (on the application of Tracey) v Cambridge University Hospitals NHS Foundation Trust* [2014] EWCA Civ 822, [2015] Q.B. 543, [2014] 3 W.L.R. 1054, [2015] 1 All E.R. 450. In *Winspear* the court held that the core principle of prior consultation applied before a decision not to attempt CPR was put into place. If it was both practicable and appropriate to consult then in the absence of some other compelling reason against consultation, the decision to file the notice on the patient's medical records would be procedurally flawed as it would not meet the requirements of s.4(7). It would not be in accordance with the law and would be an interference with article 8(1) that was not justified under article 8(2). The trust argued that the registrar had reasonably believed that the notice would be in the son's best interests under s.5(1)(b) of the Act. However, a "best interests" decision meant something broader than clinical judgement and normally required consultation. The trust had breached its duty under s.4(7) and there was no s.5(2) defence to the claim. The trust had violated its procedural duty under article 8(2). However, the mother was not entitled to just satisfaction by a personal claim for damages. Her legitimate interest was as the son's carer, and it was his best interests and right to respect for private life that had been under consideration. A declaration that there had been a procedural breach of article 8 was sufficient satisfaction for the mother as the notice had no impact on the son's actual treatment (see paras 63-64). The patient, via his mother, was thus entitled to a declaration but not to damages.

15 Under the Mental Capacity (Amendment) Act 2019, which extends to England and Wales, DOLS will be replaced by Liberty Protection Safeguards (LPS) which will streamline deprivations of liberty. Whether this provides sufficient protection for patients remains to be seen. The meaning of "deprivation of liberty" has been clarified and simplified by the Supreme Court in the case of *Cheshire West and Chester Council v P* ("the Cheshire West case") [2014] UKSC 19 [2014] A.C. 896, [2014] 2 W.L.R. 642. [2014] 2 All E.R. 585.

16 See again *Winspear v City Hospitals Sunderland NHS Foundation Trust* [2015] EWHC 3250 (QB), [2016] Q.B. 691, [2016] 2 W.L.R. 1089, *op cit.*

17 [2018] EWCOP 36.

18 [2011] EWHC 1377 (COP).

19 See again *Winspear v City Hospitals Sunderland NHS Foundation Trust* [2015] EWHC 3250 (QB), [2016] Q.B. 691, [2016] 2 W.L.R. 1089, *op cit.*

20 *Care of dying adults in the last days of life*, Quality standard [QS144], National Institute for Health and Care Excellence, 2 March 2017.

21 *R v Adams* [1957] Crim LR 365.

22 *R v Cox* [1992] 12 BMLR 38.

23 *R v Shipman*, Preston Crown Court, January 2000.

24 "**4. False statements, &c. as to births or deaths.**
(1) If any person—
    (a) wilfully makes any false answer to any question put to him by any registrar of births or deaths relating to the particulars required to be registered concerning any birth or death, or, wilfully gives to any such registrar any false information concerning any birth or death or the cause of any death; or
    (b) wilfully makes any false certificate or declaration under or for the purposes of any Act relating to the registration of births or deaths, or, knowing any such certificate or declaration to be false, uses the same as true or gives or sends the same as true to any person; or
    (c) wilfully makes, gives or uses any false statement or declaration as to a child born alive as having been still-born, or as to the body of a deceased person or a still-born child in any coffin, or falsely pretends that any child born alive was still-born; or
    (d) makes any false statement with intent to have the same inserted in any register of births or deaths:
he shall be guilty of a misdemeanour..."

25 *Guidance for doctors completing Medical Certificates of Cause of Death in England and Wales*, Office for National Statistics, 25 March 2022.

26 SI 1112 of 2019.

27 SI 2088 of 1987.

28 See here: https://www.england.nhs.uk/establishing-medical-examiner-system-nhs/

Call for Remedial Actions

Sam H. Ahmedzai, James Bogle, Denise Charlesworth-Smith,
Robert S. Harris and Lynda Rose

Why do we need a call for remedial actions?

As our starting point on undertaking this Report, we believed that delivery of professional end of life care across Britain is mostly compassionate and effective. However, in this Report we present evidence of the shocking consequences when end of life care "goes wrong".

More than six hundred families forming the support group cited in the Background supplied us with distressing patient and family experiences. We can therefore only suspect that the sixteen case studies we have selected and discussed in detail here represent just the "tip of the iceberg" in terms of breaches of duty of care.

The Care Quality Commission (CQC) and the National Institute for Health and Care Excellence (NICE) have also published independent reports which quantify the extent to which end of life care has been seen to fall short of their standards and guidelines, respectively, since the abolition of the LCP (CQC, 2016; NICE, 2020).

National audits of end of life care undertaken by the Royal College of Physicians (RCP) and more recently by the current National Audit of Care at the End of Life (NACEL) programme have also shown where there are deficiencies, but these have focused mostly on deaths in hospitals and more recently, mental health in-patient trusts (RCP, 2016; NACEL, 2022).[1] Thus, the standard of care given to people in the last days of life is evidently variable and, if found wanting, causes significant distress to many patients and to those important to them. We do not know whether the variability is "random" or whether it arises in specific healthcare settings or in particular parts of the country.

It is ten years since the publication of "More Care, Less Pathway" (LCP Review panel, 2013), and eight years since the publication of the NICE guideline NG31 (NICE, 2015). Both recommended the adoption of individualised care plans and prescribing. Regrettably, we do not know to what extent hospital trusts, hospices, nursing and care homes and general practices have actually taken up the new guidance, or whether they are still following LCP principles under a new name. However, we do know from many of our case studies that elements of the "one size fits all" and "blanket" approaches – especially with respect to unilateral withholding of hydration – are still encountered by patients and their loved ones. We strongly suspect that the cases we have uncovered are examples of what may be widespread poor practices and a failure to take proper cognizance of the LCP review, NICE guidelines and pre-existing GMC guidance (2010).

We have also seen that when end of life care did go wrong, it was very hard for the people who were on the receiving end – patients and families – to raise complaints and be taken seriously. In theory the hospital Patient Advice and Liaison Service (PALS)[2] is supposed to be available for all sorts of clinical complaints and no doubt it is effective for simpler grievances. But there is nowhere for people to turn for rapid advice and help, specifically at the time negligent end of life care treatments are being experienced.

After a death, the Parliamentary and Health Service Ombudsman[3] is one avenue for addressing grievances and this office's input can be helpful in identifying poor clinical practice (see case study 4). However, in some cases the PHSO may decline to respond because of a time delay (see case study 9). Moreover, the PHSO, has no powers to bring civil cases or prosecutions even when, following investigation, it finds evidence of malpractice.[4]

Some complainants have been fortunate to have coroners' inquests that can issue findings on serious malpractice contributing to death and specifically identify those responsible (case study 7). But we suspect that the majority of families are too stressed or overwhelmed with grief to pursue complaints (case studies 9, 13) or would not have the resources to fund a lengthy fight through the courts (case study 2). Many will simply have nowhere to turn for help and understanding.

Of the various non-litigious methods of attempting to obtain relief or redress of grievance, all too often, as can be seen from many of the case studies, they are simply not working.

Going down the route of litigation is expensive and can also be unsatisfactory since it is necessarily adversarial when, much of the time, a non-adversarial approach might be better and lead to a less defensive approach being taken by NHS trusts and clinical staff.

Additionally, fatal accident legislation, which incorporates actions for assault, is now very out of date and not really fit for purpose in a modern NHS clinical setting. The Fatal Accidents Act 1976 and the Law Reform (Miscellaneous Provisions) Act 1934 are both considerably out of date, have become somewhat clumsy means of obtaining redress and the awards are very small.

The bringing of criminal proceedings against an NHS trust or clinicians is a very serious matter and could have very serious consequences in the event of a finding of guilt. It is, alas, clear that this route, on the evidence available to our experts, could be indicated in some of the case studies we cite. However we believe it is essential that effective forms of relief and redress be in place which need not necessarily entail criminal proceedings. At present, as stated above and as seen from the various case studies, these other forms of review, relief and redress have often become defensive, inadequate and even ineffective. That is clearly very unsatisfactory and requires prompt and effective remedy, but this is beyond the scope of the present Report.

It is also not our place to make new clinical recommendations or issue new guidance on the delivery of care, which are the domain of government bodies like NICE or professional bodies such as the General Medical Council, General Nursing and Midwifery Council and the Royal Colleges. On the other hand, serious malpractice should not be allowed to continue. So we are proposing some specific actions, at national, regional or local levels, which we believe could make a difference to those who have suffered – or who are currently suffering – poor care, by attending to the persistent concerns highlighted above.

What actions are needed?

From the evidence we have reviewed and our understanding of current clinical guidelines and legal routes, we are proposing six remedies which, if implemented, we believe can rapidly and effectively reduce the level of malpractice occurring in care at the end of life, or mitigate its harm.

1. We call for a national inventory of end of life care plans, policies and procedures currently being used in all healthcare settings

We propose that there should be a mandatory nationwide inventory of what end of life care systems and procedures UK healthcare providers have introduced to replace the LCP. This national stock-taking should not just list the names of current policies and procedures, because some of these may still hide discredited LCP-influenced practices – therefore the body conducting the inventory should be empowered to identify the specific components of what is actually delivered. There should be a standardised system for categorising the actual delivery of end of life care according to the "5 Priorities for Care" (2014) and the seventy two recommendations of the NICE guideline NG31. Failure to adopt, deviation from, and watering down of these priorities and guidelines should be readily identifiable against each healthcare provider in the inventory. We would include both statutory NHS providers and also third sector services such as hospices, and it should also cover private facilities.

We understand this is a very large undertaking, but we believe after the first review, subsequent updates would only be needed at intervals, say after updates to national guidance. We consider that the National Institute for Health and Care Research (NIHR) could invite bids from universities and independent organisations to conduct and report the survey. Some of the data could be sought by a large, coordinated Freedom of Information request. The selected organisation should have access to findings of the CQC, Healthcare Quality Improvement Partnership (HQIP) and NACEL exercises.

This **"National End of Life Care Policies and Procedures Inventory"** should be publicly available, in formats which are accessible to both lay people and healthcare professionals, and in a range of languages.

Funding for such a large undertaking could be from a research grant awarded by the NIHR or it could be supported by NICE as part of its oversight of national guidelines (NICE, 2020).

2. *We propose a national rapid response service to advise and support people who have a loved one currently experiencing poor quality end of life care*

We propose that there should be a free-to-access, rapid response, independent service across the United Kingdom, to which people can turn for real-time advice and support when their loved one is being treated as being in the last days of life but they are experiencing a poor quality of care. This could address the scenarios – which all of our case studies have highlighted – of end of life care going wrong and where the healthcare provider is failing to respond to the patient's and family concerns.

In cases where the patient is identified as having diminished capacity to make his or her own end of life decisions, we acknowledge that the current facility to appoint an Independent Mental Capacity Advocate (IMCA) can be very helpful in working with the clinical team and carers to resolve disputes. However, in case study 7 we noted that the coroner robustly criticised the hospital trust for its complete failure to observe the Mental Capacity Act 2005 and the rights of the patient, who was clearly lacking capacity, or of her parents. The proposed rapid response team may be instrumental in alerting families and healthcare staff to the need for an IMCA.

Moreover, many of the other case studies featured patients who may have had capacity to make decisions but these, and their family advocates, were not being heard, or were being over-ruled by clinicians.

PALS may help in some cases in hospital, but we are concerned that their staff may not have the expertise or capacity to advise, in a timely fashion, on critical or highly complex end of life situations. Also, PALS services do not apply for patients in hospices, care homes or in their own homes.

As we have shown, there may be doubt about whether the patient is indeed at the end of life or is experiencing an acute temporary deterioration of a chronic condition. GMC gave guidance to doctors in the latter scenario and NICE guideline NG31 gave recommendations on how clinical teams should assess the possibility of dying, and the need to monitor daily to look for changes such as stabilising or improvement (GMC, 2010; NICE NG31, 2015); but we found many cases where these recommendations were not followed. Using information provided by the families, the proposed rapid response service could either give reassurance that the person is indeed dying, or – where necessary – could raise legitimate questions for family members to take to the clinicians.

Where it is clear and accepted by all that the person is indeed in the last days of life, the rapid response service could check what information the family members have been given about current treatments, compare against current guidelines and, if the current care being offered appears to fall short of best practice, give speedy feedback on further specific questions for them to put to the clinical team.

We acknowledge that this national **"Rapid Response Service for End of**

Life Crises" is potentially a huge undertaking. It is unlikely, in our opinion, that the NHS itself would have the resources and the independence to provide this service. Instead, we envisage teams of trained and knowledgeable volunteers and professionals providing *pro bono* advice and support by telephone, in the same way as the Samaritans and Childline. For those with access to suitable technology, the service could also be provided by email or virtual meetings. We believe there are many retired healthcare professionals – ideally but not necessarily with end of life care clinical experience – who could give a few hours a week or month to support this service. To make it more manageable and responsive, the service could be regional, e.g. based on an Integrated Care Board, in keeping with its newly statutory obligation to palliative and end of life care (Health and Care Act 2022).

Funding, even for a volunteer-based service, is likely to be an issue. This Report has identified the problems and the case of need, but we seek advice from Parliamentarians on how to fund such a service.

3. We propose setting up a fast track advice helpline for recently bereaved families

We propose that a logical extension to the "Rapid Response Service for End of Life Crises", which is for families of people currently being treated at the end of life, is to support those who have recently been bereaved but have grievances about the quality of care. We have noted, sadly, that many of our case study informants were unable to pursue these complaints because of lack of knowledge and administrative delays.

The end of life care support group described in case study 1 and set up by one of the contributors to this report, Mrs Denise Charlesworth-Smith, has proved to be hugely successful, gathering to date over six hundred individuals and families affected by poor end of life care – mainly by word of mouth and social media. This is admirable, but it is clearly unsustainable for one individual to give so much support.

We therefore propose a national **"Fast Track Advice Helpline for Recently Bereaved Families"**, comprising teams of specialists and laypeople, who could be available on a voluntary basis to give telephone, virtual online or email advice. Such teams could include retired healthcare and legal professionals. Laypeople – especially those who have been affected by poor end of life care themselves – could be involved, with support and supervision. The hospice movement has shown the power of volunteers who are trained and supported.

This "Fast Track Advice Helpline for recently bereaved families" would therefore be related to, and ideally work in parallel with, the "Rapid Response Service for End of Life Crises" proposed above. Similarly, the helpline could be organised regionally, e.g. based on an Integrated Care Board.

Usually the advice and support would amount to signposting available expertise or to the proposed National Register (see below). We hope that charities for specific illnesses, such as cancer, or dementia or for people with learning disabilities, could be persuaded to offer financial assistance and training.

4. We call for a national register of cases where end of life care has fallen below standards or breaches guidelines

Our starting point and continuing belief is that end of life care is mostly of a very high standard across the United Kingdom. However, the shocking cases described in this Report show that we cannot take this for granted. We are therefore proposing the setting up of a national register of cases, where end of life care which has "gone wrong" can be submitted – as they arise – by members of the public or professionals. Ideally this should be hosted by one of the national healthcare regulatory agencies such as CQC or HQIP, who are already involved in monitoring and regulating the quality of end of life care on a cyclical basis. Alternatively, it could be placed with one of the professional bodies, such as the Royal College of Physicians.

We recommend that families and clinicians should be able to upload cases to this **"National Quality of End of Life Care Register"** as soon as possible after they have arisen, through paper forms or a user-friendly secure website. When we refer to the role of families here, we do not envisage that they would upload clinical documents; rather, their contribution would be to put a spotlight on deaths that they believe warrant investigation. It could be that while the person was still alive, the "Rapid Response Service for End of Life Crises" (call for action 2 above) or – after a death - the "Fast track advice helpline for recently bereaved families" (call for action 3 above) may have been involved and existing documentation from these could help the families to upload their concerns.

On the other side of the Register, the cases that have been uploaded should be accessible confidentially by regulatory bodies, the police, the Ombudsman and coroners.

Regarding the role of the Ombudsman, we find it anomalous that the PHSO is unable to initiate legal proceedings if it is found that negligence has contributed to death. We would therefore ask Parliament to consider the need to grant the PHSO the power to initiate prosecutions.

To be effective, we propose that the Register should publish an annual semi-anonymised report, giving details of the collated national statistics of poor end of life care. Some of the individual cases could be highlighted, as we have done with the case studies in the Report. By semi-anonymised we mean that the register would not contain names of specific patients, family members, or individual clinicians or health managers associated with the cases; but the settings – whether hospital, hospice, care or nursing home or GP practices would be identifiable. This is in keeping with the way that the Royal Colleges, HQIP and CQC publish their national audits and inquiries. These annual reports should be digitally accessible to the public; those working in the NHS, hospices and care homes; regulatory bodies such as CQC; the Ombudsman – and of course by Parliament.

5. We call for the urgent adoption of a uniform national system to capture patients' preferences for end of life care

A salient feature of many of our case studies is the variability in the way that patients (and their family members, including those who hold an LPA) are allowed to express and record their preferences for end of life care – or excluded from this. The commonest aspect that has caused so much concern is regarding DNACPR decisions. Often, these were made apparently unilaterally by doctors, without reference to family members and even to those holding an LPA.

Another source of distress was the way that patients were denied nutrition and/or hydration, again often without the patient's expressed consent or families' involvement.

A third concern is the assumption of some patients and families that accepting a DNACPR decision would inevitably lead to withdrawal of nutrition, hydration, and other comfort measures (see case study 10).

Across the United Kingdom, there is a multiplicity of ways that patients' advanced decisions (also called "advanced directives" or "advance care plans") are captured and recorded. In order to reduce this variability the

Resuscitation Council UK has led the development of a uniform way of recording what is important to the patient. in case of becoming suddenly gravely ill. (Hawkes et al, 2020)[5] This process is called the Recommended Summary Plan for Emergency Care and Treatment (ReSPECT)[6] – see Appendix 8. ReSPECT is encapsulated in a two-page plan which is completed and signed by the patient after a detailed discussion with healthcare professionals. It allows for preferences to be recorded about CPR but also whether hydration, nutrition, antibiotics and escalation to ITU are desired by the patient, if the situation arises. ReSPECT does not replace a more wide-ranging ACP but can form an important part of it. It is presently undergoing evaluation and testing in different settings, and the Resuscitation Council is continually updating the plan and its supporting documentation in response to this research.

Our proposal is for a **"Uniform national system of recording patients' preferences at end of life"**, based on the ReSPECT process, but including other recognised approaches to capturing patients' end of life choices such as advanced care plans. We recommend that the latest version of the ReSPECT plan is rapidly incorporated into care pathways for all chronically ill people and especially those who are likely to be approaching end of life in the coming months and years. We also support the recommendation of the Resuscitation Council that universal use of ReSPECT should be added to the Palliative and End of Life guidance for the Integrated Care Boards under the Health and Care Act 2022.

6. *We propose further high quality research into social, medical and nursing aspects of end of life care*

The LCP Review panel and NICE guidelines have made calls for more research to improve care in the last days of life. The NIHR and charities, such as Marie Curie and those for neurological conditions, have put out calls for large (i.e. over £1 million) research projects. We welcome these grants which are usually won by large teams of postdoctoral level academics.

But we believe there is also scope for issuing a larger number of smaller grants to support health and social care students at undergraduate or Master's level (under the supervision of respected academic departments), to perform many more projects in local communities.

These projects could explore reasons why end of life care fails in specific settings, e.g. for people with deprived or ethnic backgrounds, learning disabilities, etc. Ideally such studies should be co-designed and co-produced with lay people affected by these issues. They would also lend themselves to an 'action research' methodology where results are immediately fed back into the relevant communities.

A further stimulus to these smaller scale research studies is the rise of "compassionate communities"[7] as part of the global movement to open up discussions about death and dying in society.

Moving from Calls to Action

The six calls for remedial actions outlined above are aspirational, as although the LCFCPG wishes this Report to go beyond just describing cases of poor end of life care, we do not have the remit or capacity to enact them. Specifically, we do not presently have a ready business plan or costing for these calls for action. We envisage that the Royal Colleges, NICE, NIHR and independent research charities take a lead on developing some of these actions.

At this stage, we wish to reach out to Parliamentarians, so that, by highlighting current and continuing deficiencies and failures, we may facilitate restoration of the good care that has, until relatively recently, been a hallmark of NHS provision and practice.

---

[1] NACEL measures the performance of hospitals against criteria relating to the five priorities, and relevant *NICE Guideline (NG31)* and *Quality Standards (QS13 and QS144)*. https://www.nhsbenchmarking.nhs.uk/nacel-audit-outputs

[2] https://www.nhs.uk/nhs-services/hospitals/what-is-pals-patient-advice-and-liaison-service/

[3] https://www.ombudsman.org.uk

[4] S.3 Health Service Commissioners Act 1993.

[5] One of the contributors to this report, Professor Emeritus Sam H Ahmedzai was a co-author of this publication of ReSPECT.

[6] ReSPECT has evolved from what are called Treatment Escalation Plans (TEP) or Emergency Care and Treatment plans (ECTP).

[7] For an example of an approach to compassionate communities in the United Kingdom see: http://compassionate-communities.co.uk

Compendium of terms

This Compendium has been compiled from key terms used in this Report, or concepts which can have an impact on how end of life care is delivered, but which are often misunderstood or subject to misconceptions by professionals as well as lay people. We have gone beyond supplying a "dictionary definition" in order to set the terminology in the context of end of life care and referring, when appropriate, to specific case studies in which these terms are highly relevant.

Cardiopulmonary resuscitation (CPR) and DNACPR decisions

The term CPR consists of three key parts: "cardio" meaning heart and circulation, "pulmonary" meaning lungs and breathing, and "resuscitation" which means the correction of sudden failure of those two organs, in order to continue life. CPR is most likely to benefit a patient if there is cardiac arrest (the heart suddenly stops circulating blood); or if there is respiratory arrest (the lungs suddenly stop inflating).

If the heart arrests, resuscitation by external massage to the chest to keep the circulation going and, if facilities are available, giving electric shocks externally via paddles on the chest (using a defibrillator) can, in the right circumstances, correct the heart's electrical rhythm and restore good circulation. If normal breathing fails, resuscitation can take the form of blowing air into the windpipe to inflate the lungs. Often these interventions are done together.

CPR is much less likely to help in people with progressive multiple organ failure, advanced cancer or advanced frailty where death occurs gradually and is a natural end to a chronic illness. In older frail people, chest massage can cause broken ribs and be distressing for patients and their relatives to watch. Avoiding CPR in these situations may allow for a more dignified death.

Therefore, the decision to offer CPR or not must always be made on an individual basis. Patients can opt out of CPR and doctors must honour that. But patients cannot insist on having CPR – that is something a doctor must ultimately decide, considering the likelihood of it working and of potential harms. Current General Medical Council (GMC) guidance recommends doctors to consult with each patient, or: "If a patient lacks capacity to make a decision about future CPR, you must consult those close to the patient as part of the decision making process." (General Medical Council, 2010; see also Appendix 4.)

DNACPR stands for "Do Not Attempt Cardiopulmonary Resuscitation". It is a specific part of the management plan placed into a patient's records after the discussion referred to above. Ideally a doctor, patient and possibly family members will have come to an agreement as to whether the patient would benefit from CPR, or whether the risks of harm outweigh any benefit. If the patient lacks mental capacity to make the decision, doctors have a duty to seek someone close to them who may hold power of attorney for such health decisions. If there is no such person, a "Best Interests" meeting may be called to come to a balanced decision.

It is important to understand that making a DNACPR decision does not mean that other forms of supportive and comfort measures for the patient could be withheld by staff. These include nutrition and hydration (see below), or antibiotics. Recently, a new process called ReSPECT has become available in the UK which allows patients, doctors and possibly family members to make a written plan that can stipulate which of these supportive and comfort measures are wanted, as well as a CPR decision (Hawkes et al, 2020; see also Appendix 8).

[Case studies 3, 9, 10, 12, 13, 14]

Duty of Care

All clinicians and health care staff have a duty of care toward the patients whom they have been tasked with treating or nursing.

The modern definition of a duty of care arose out of the law of negligence and gives rise to civil claims for clinical negligence, to be distinguished from claims in criminal law e.g. manslaughter, assault and battery and so on (although assault can also give rise to a civil claim, the standard of proof required is higher in a criminal claim).

In simple terms, to establish that there has been clinical negligence for which a doctor, or his or her employer, such as the Trust or Hospice, is liable, the claimant must establish that there has been a breach of the duty of care and that it caused the harm suffered, without any break in the chain of causation, and that the harm caused is not too remote from the cause.

In clinical negligence cases, it is a defence for the clinician to show that he or she has acted in accordance with a practice accepted as proper by a responsible body of medical men and women skilled in that particular form of treatment (the so-called "Bolam" test of negligence).[1]

This, however, may not always be sufficient, and the court has to satisfy itself that the medical experts could point to a logical basis for the opinion they were supporting. Where cases concern the balancing of risks against benefits, the court has to be sure that, in forming their opinion, the medical experts have considered the issue of comparative risks and benefits and have reached a view which can be defended. This is the so-called "Bolitho test" of negligence.[2]

End of life care plans, packages and pathways

Care plans are present throughout health and social care, covering birth to death. They have also been called "packages", "pathways" or "protocols". The benefit of using a care plan is that (a) the team agrees and records what the patient will receive, and (b) the components of the care plan are ideally based on research or other reliable evidence.

Plans specifically for overseeing good quality care at the end of life started to emerge in the 1980s. The Liverpool Care Pathway (LCP) was devised in the 1990s specifically with the intention of spreading experience of achieving a "good death" as practised in UK hospices, into NHS hospitals, nursing and care homes as well as people's own homes. For detailed analyses of why the LCP ultimately failed and had to be abolished, see the Preface, Foreword and Background, and Appendix 7 to this Report.

Following the LCP's abolition, end of life care plans and packages still exist in many different forms. Some are designed to help identify when a person may be entering the end of life phase of a chronic illness such as cancer, for example the AMBER care bundle.[3] Others go beyond recognition of dying and include multiprofessional aspects of care and attention to psychological and spiritual wellbeing of patients and families, such as the Gold Standards Framework.[4] Both of these packages could apply within the last months or years of life. It is relevant to point out that, although currently used in the NHS, so far neither of these has been subject to independent full-scale clinical trials.

Considering plans and pathways for the very last days of life, the LCP review panel recommended that care plans for dying people should be individualised. (LCP review panel, 2013; see also Appendix 1) This became a key part of the "Five priorities for care" (Leadership Alliance for the Care of Dying People, 2014; see also Appendix 2) and the NICE guideline NG31 (2015); see also Appendix 3. However, there is a concern that despite the national recommendations, in some parts of the NHS and in care and nursing homes and hospices, the basic practices of the LCP continue to be used but under a different name.

There has been no national inventory of all the different care plans, pathways and protocols used for the last days of life across the UK, and to what extent they comply with national guidelines.

[Case studies 1, 2, 3, 5, 6, 7, 9, 10, 11, 12, 15, 16]

Medical futility and burdensomeness, at the end of life

Futility and burdensomeness in healthcare and specifically in medical decision-making is a poorly understood topic that is probably not taught well to medical, nursing and other healthcare staff. It is partly an ethical issue, partly clinical. It is therefore not possible to talk generically about all instances of medical futility and burdensomeness – each situation must be weighed up individually. Essentially, if a treatment is judged to be 'futile' it can have no possible value to the patient; whereas if a treatment is 'burdensome' it will either become a burden personally to the patient, or the use of resources cannot be justified.

At the end of life, decisions about these issues may be especially complex because of the added dimension that a decision may have life or death consequences within hours or days.

The law has been quite specific and direct on the subjects of futility and burdensomeness. In the UK Supreme Court case of *Aintree University Hospitals NHS Foundation Trust v James,*[5] Baroness Hale summarised the Court's views in the case of extending the life of a person who had been receiving intensive care for many months but the hospital wanted to withdraw life-supporting treatment on grounds of alleged "futility" of treatment (see case study 2). She said: "A treatment may bring some benefit to the patient even though it has no effect upon the underlying disease or disability." [6]

This clearly means that even if embarking on (or continuing) a treatment in a dying person may have little chance of extending life or restoring "health", it may nevertheless be worthwhile (and hence not futile) from the patient's viewpoint. This may be because the treatment is felt by the patient to be important for relief (or prevention) of pain or other kinds of suffering.

These issues are often unnecessarily confused by those who attempt to elide the meaning of the words "futility" and "burdensomeness" of treatment, with a "quality of life" judgment about the value of a person's life, whether to themselves or to others. Treatments may be futile and burdensome, but that is not the same as saying that the patient's life is futile or burdensome, which is a purely subjective judgment that can only, ultimately, be made by the patient. (See Compendium entry under 'Quality of life' for more on this aspect.)

[Case studies 2, 3, 4, 10]

Medication at the end of life

Patients at the end of life are frequently prescribed medications by a variety of routes. We cannot cover them all, but two which are frequently cited in our case studies, and which also were the focus of concern for the LCP Review panel, are morphine and midazolam.

Morphine

Morphine is very well known as a painkiller. Many also understand that it is derived from the opium plant, which is why morphine and chemically similar drugs are called "opioids". The fact that morphine is one of the world's oldest drugs (known to be used by the ancient Egyptians) is not a justification for its use in all cases of severe pain. Morphine and its derivative diamorphine, also known as heroin, were recommended drugs in UK end of life care by NICE guideline CG140 (published 2012 and last updated 2016), not necessarily because of pharmacological advantages, but primarily because of their cheapness and familiarity to prescribers. (NICE, 2016)

Morphine can control all but the most extreme pain encountered in end of life scenarios, but unfortunately these are the scenarios where its side effects are most troublesome. Morphine is a sedative, which may be helpful in some circumstances, but it can cause such sedation that patients lose the ability to communicate with staff and family members. Skilled specialist doctors know how to regulate the dose to minimise sedation; many others do not, and undue sedation was a frequently reported issue for patients who died while on the LCP.

Other very common side effects of morphine include nausea and vomiting, dry mouth, constipation, bladder retention, and respiratory depression. The latter is the reason why morphine and other opioids must only be used with caution in patients with chronic lung disease such as chronic bronchitis or emphysema. Moreover, in any patient, at too high – or too quickly escalated – a dose, morphine can cause respiratory arrest.

If there is kidney failure (which is not uncommon at the end of life), morphine's by-products are not effectively removed from the body, so that serious adverse effects such as agitation, hallucinations and even – paradoxically – increased pain can emerge.

Morphine is reasonably well absorbed by mouth but for patients who cannot swallow, it can be given through a tube placed in the stomach via the nose (nasogastric tube), or by injection or infusion. Injections can be intravenous (into a vein), the most reliable route and easy to give in hospital and some hospices; or subcutaneous (just under the skin), the preferred way in hospices or at home because of its ease for nurses, who do not usually give intravenous injections in the UK.

For patients who need more than 2-3 injections in a day, NICE guideline NG31 (2015) recommends placing the estimated dose for the next 24 hours into a battery-powered syringe driver and giving it as an infusion. (See Appendix 3.) This is called a continuous subcutaneous infusion (CSCI). Overuse of CSCIs of morphine – often started too early and with the dose escalating too fast, leading to an unresponsive patient and possibly an accelerated death – was one of the complaints arising from misuse of the LCP.

Midazolam

Midazolam is, by contrast to morphine, a very modern drug, not derived from a plant but manufactured industrially. It is primarily a sedative, belonging to the class of medicines called benzodiazepines, of which very many are used in healthcare for anxiety reduction, aiding sleep, reducing agitation and preventing epileptic seizures (fits).

It is usually given to adults by intravenous or subcutaneous injection and has the effect of reducing anxiety and agitation within seconds. It has become very much used in end of life care for just these reasons – rapid relaxation and reduction of agitation and fits. Midazolam by itself has little effect on pain (other than by virtue of its sedative effect), but it may reduce the distress of severe breathing problems at the end of life. Unfortunately, as with morphine, if the prescriber is not experienced it is relatively easy to cause over-sedation. Also, as with morphine, midazolam can depress the control of breathing so it can lead to respiratory arrest in susceptible individuals, or, at too high a dose, even in healthy people.

The combination of morphine (or other strong opioid drugs such as oxycodone or fentanyl) with midazolam is commonly prescribed at the end of life, often delivered together by CSCI. In expert hands, the combination is safe and able to give pain control and ease of anxiety and agitation; but with less skilled staff, and especially if continuous infusions of the two drugs are started too early and not monitored, they may lead to hastening of death.

[Case studies 1, 3, 5, 6, 12, 13, 15]

Mental incapacity and the Mental Capacity Act 2005

The treatment, care and rights of the mentally incapacitated was dealt with comprehensively by the Mental Capacity Act 2005.

S.2 defines those who lack capacity as those unable to make a decision because of impairment or disturbance of the function of the mind or brain.

Formal assessments of mental incapacity are carried out by doctors and have to follow specific guidance from the NHS on the application of the Mental Capacity Act 2005, which states that:

"Someone can lack capacity to make some decisions (for example, to decide on complex financial issues) but still have the capacity to make other decisions (for example, to decide what items to buy at the local shop)."

"The MCA says:

• assume a person has the capacity to make a decision themselves, unless it's proved otherwise

• wherever possible, help people to make their own decisions

• do not treat a person as lacking the capacity to make a decision just because they make an unwise decision

• if you make a decision for someone who does not have capacity, it must be in their best interests

• treatment and care provided to someone who lacks capacity should be the least restrictive of their basic rights and freedoms

The MCA also allows people to express their preferences for care and treatment, and to appoint a trusted person to make a decision on their behalf should they lack capacity in the future." [7]

Clinicians also receive guidance from NICE on assessing conditions such as delirium which may impair mental capacity, in its Clinical Knowledge Summaries 2021.[8]

Under s.4, all must be done for the "best interests" of the patient and the patient's past and present wishes and feelings, and beliefs and values, must be considered and any appointed welfare attorney or advance statement taken into account.

Under Part 2 of the Act, the Court of Protection ceased to be an administrative office and became a fully functioning court to decide matters relating to mental capacity and mentally incapacitated patients.

Ss. 9-14 make provisions for legally binding welfare and financial powers of attorney. Under a welfare power of attorney, the medical "attorney" nominated by the patient can, in accordance with the terms of the power of attorney, refuse clinical treatment as if he or she were the patient and clinicians are bound to accede to the attorney's wishes, even if the patient dies as a result. It is accordingly important how the document is drafted and whom the patient has appointed as his or her attorney. The document only comes into force when the patient has been clearly assessed to be mentally incapacitated. If there is genuine doubt that the document represents the patient's true current wishes there may be scope to challenge the document in court.

Ss. 24-26 make provisions for legally binding advance decisions to refuse treatment which clinicians are bound to obey, even though they may have been made years in advance when the patient was not suffering from the relevant conditions. The document only comes into force when the patient has been clearly assessed to be mentally incapacitated. However, if there is doubt that the advance statement represents the patient's current will, it may be possible to challenge the document in court.

Ss. 35-41 of the Act also set up independent mental capacity advocates to assist and advise in such cases.

Under the Mental Capacity (Amendment) Act 2019, which extends to England and Wales, the deprivation of liberty safeguards (DOLS) and orders, currently in force under the Mental Capacity Act, will be replaced by Liberty Protection Safeguards (LPS) which will streamline deprivations of liberty.

These orders are misnamed since they are primarily orders precisely to *remove* a patient's liberty where the court is persuaded that, if liberty is not removed, then the patient may be in danger of harming himself or herself e.g. by discharging himself or herself from hospital. Whether the new LPS system provides sufficient protection for patients remains to be seen.

[Case studies 2, 7, 8, 10, 14]

Nutrition and hydration

Nutrition and hydration are both essential for life, but of the two, hydration is more critical. If all food intake is stopped, but adequate hydration is continued, a person will become increasingly weak and frail and suffer hunger pangs until death ensues within weeks. But if hydration is completely stopped, then most people can only survive for a few days. Dying from lack of hydration is also distressing, with symptoms including thirst, dry and cracked mouth preventing speech and swallowing, headache, lethargy, muscle weakness, confusion, agitation and ultimately loss of consciousness.

If a patient near to end of life loses the ability to swallow any kind of food, adequate nutrition can still be given indefinitely if medically appropriate and desired by the patient. Although receiving food and water is a basic human right and a universal comfort measure, if it has to be given by "artificial" means, the fitting and maintenance of the tube is presently regarded as a 'medical treatment' and needs to be authorised by a doctor, in case there could be any adverse medical consequences. Reciprocally, a doctor and a court have the authority to withhold or withdraw the artificial means of nutrition and hydration (GMC, 2010).[9]

However, if the patient can still be given hydration and nutrition orally then the obligation to sustain the patient remains. If the patient cannot be fed or hydrated orally, then, under the current law, if artificial means are ordered to be withdrawn, the patient will inevitably die of dehydration. It is fair to say that although this is the current law and guidance from GMC, it is widely questioned by many, both within and outside the medical profession, on clinical and ethical grounds. It seems to be a clear infringement of the prime ethical principle "first do no harm".

Furthermore, the guidance from GMC is fully consistent with this view. It states:

"109. All patients are entitled to food and drink of adequate quantity and quality and to the help they need to eat and drink… You must keep the nutrition and hydration status of your patients under review. You should be satisfied that nutrition and hydration are being provided in a way that meets your patients' needs, and that if necessary, patients are being given adequate help to enable them to eat and drink.

"110. If a patient needs assistance in eating or drinking that is not being provided, or if underlying problems are not being effectively managed, you should take steps to rectify the situation, if you can. If you cannot, you should inform an appropriate person within the organisation that is responsible for the patient's care."

"112. Clinically assisted hydration can also be provided by intravenous or subcutaneous infusion of fluids through a 'drip'. <u>The terms 'clinically assisted nutrition' and 'clinically assisted hydration' do not refer to help given to patients to eat or drink, for example by spoon feeding</u>."

(Our underlining) (GMC, 2010, updated 2022; see also Appendix 4).

NICE guideline NG31 also supports this commonsense and humane position, namely that if a person at the end of life wishes to drink but is unable, then they should be supported to do so, enlisting the help of family members if available:

"1.4.1 Support the dying person to drink if they wish to and are able to. Check for any difficulties, such as swallowing problems or risk of aspiration. Discuss the risks and benefits of continuing to drink, with the dying person, and those involved in the dying person's care.

"1.4.2 Offer frequent care of the mouth and lips to the dying person, and include the management of dry mouth in their care plan, if needed. Offer the person the following, as needed:

• help with cleaning their teeth or dentures, if they would like

• frequent sips of fluid.

"<u>1.4.3 Encourage people important to the dying person to help with mouth and lip care or giving drinks, if they wish to. Provide any necessary aids and give them advice on giving drinks safely</u>."

(Our underlining) (NICE NG31 2015; see also Appendix 3).

Thus it is compatible with the law, GMC and NICE guidance that people who are at the end of life who wish to remain hydrated, should be offered oral fluids as long as it is not causing a medical risk (i.e. following a formal swallow assessment) – regardless of whether they are receiving clinically assisted hydration (or nutrition) or even if these have been withdrawn.

This point has been stressed because several of our case studies highlight the inevitable tension that arises between the humane requests, from both patients and family members, for hydration at the end of life, against what may be seen as a form of medical paternalism when clinicians deny these reasonable and humane requests.

Methods of 'clinically assisted' nutrition or hydration include passing a narrow tube through the nose into the stomach (nasogastric or NG tube), or via the abdominal wall directly into the stomach (called a PEG or PEJ tube depending on where it enters the gut). Simple fluids or complex nutritious feeds can be given this way and many people can live comfortably with PEG or PEJ tubes for months, for example after a stroke. Moreover, the fitting of an NG tube is not complex and can be done by a nurse, so long as there are facilities for checking the placement of the tube by an X-Ray.

If dehydration is the immediate concern of the patient and family, then the quickest solution is to place an intravenous line in the arm (sometimes called a PICC line) to give fluids. For some people, an intravenous line may be too troublesome and so alternatively, fluids can be given subcutaneously via a small plastic needle under the skin of the abdomen or thigh. Subcutaneous fluids are very easy to set up, even in care homes, people's own homes or hospices, if the latter do not have facilities to offer intravenous fluids.

For long term feeding, an alternative to a stomach tube is intravenous or parenteral nutrition (PN), or Total PN (TPN), if all nutrition and hydration is administered this way. Again, this solution is acceptable to many patients in order to stay alive, who would otherwise have died in distress from malnutrition or dehydration, for example after a stroke, or a form of cancer that prevents eating.

Unilateral withdrawal of hydration by staff (through "nil by mouth" orders or taking down intravenous or subcutaneous fluids) was one of the major complaints brought by bereaved relatives to the LCP Review panel. This was apparently done because some staff felt that it was incompatible with a "good death" to die with such tubes fitted. Although that view is no longer tolerated, in practice patients and relatives can still experience barriers in receiving assisted forms of nutrition and hydration.

The General Medical Council (GMC, 2010) has issued clear guidance to doctors discussing these options and how to initiate and withdraw them in people who are at the end of life. The guidance explicitly differentiates how decisions are to be made for three clinical categories: 'Patients who have capacity'; 'Incapacitated adults: not expected to die in hours or days'; and 'Incapacitated adults: expected to die in hours or days'. (see Appendix 4).

[Case studies 4, 5, 6, 7, 8, 9, 10, 11, 15, 16]

Palliative care and end of life care

The Background to this Report gives a brief history of how end of life care took a major step forward from the 1960s onwards with the start of the hospice movement. It also addresses confusion about the terms currently being used in this context.

'End of life care', for the purposes of this Report, applies when a person is thought to be in the last days of life. This may be required for a person with chronic illness such as cancer or chronic heart or lung disease, or it may be needed acutely after a stroke, or other catastrophic condition. (See GMC Guidance for doctors, Appendix 4).

However, in other contexts the NHS refers to 'end of life' when a person with a chronic illness such as progressive cancer, chronic heart or lung disease or dementia is perceived to be entering the last year or so of life. This Report does not cover the care needs of that much longer period. Of course, some people who seem to have a prognosis of many months can suddenly deteriorate and enter the last days of life unexpectedly. For this reason, it is current policy for clinicians to advise people with months or years of chronic illness to make plans for this event. Advance Care Plans (ACP) are used for this purpose. These embrace other approaches such as 'advance decisions to refuse treatment' and lasting welfare powers of attorney, about DNACPR, and regarding a 'preferred place of care' or 'preferred place of death' (see Appendix 8 for more information about the ReSPECT process, which can be used as part of a broader ACP).

The term 'palliative care' is another example of words whose meaning has changed over the past decades. Initially it was coined in the 1990s as a euphemism for symptom relief and comfort measures, to avoid using the terms 'terminal' or even 'hospice' (in countries where these did not exist). Later, the medical specialty which developed from hospice care adopted this term as 'specialist palliative care', to contrast with 'generic' palliative care given by GPs and hospital staff not trained in end of life care.

[Case studies 10, 14, 16]

Principle of Double or Dual Effect

This principle, in simple terms, refers typically to a medical situation where a good or, at least ethically neutral, act is done but only a good effect is intended, albeit an unintended bad effect simultaneously and unavoidably also occurs and is foreseen. Intention is the key factor.

The classic clinical scenario is that where pain relief is administered with the intention of alleviating pain but has the unintended consequence of shortening life.

In simple terms, if the aim is to kill the pain but not the patient, the intention is not culpable, even if the unintended side-effect is that life may be shortened to a degree.

Often, however, pain relief can cause life to be lengthened, for example if the patient becomes more active and nutrition and hydration are restored, in which case the principle of double effect does not apply.

In the case of *R v Bodkin Adams*[10], the defendant claimed that he intended to alleviate pain and not to kill his patient and so argued double effect. The judge, Mr Justice Devlin, said, in summing up, where restoring a patient to health is no longer possible, a doctor may lawfully give treatment with the aim of relieving pain and suffering which, as an unintentional result, shortens life. That was an example of 'double effect'.

By contrast, in the case of *R v Dyson*[11], the court ruled that it is no defence that the patient was already dying if the defendant's conduct intentionally accelerated death. That was not 'double effect'.

Quality of life and its assessment at the end of life

The term 'quality of life' is used frequently in everyday life, but our interest in this Report is how the term is understood and used in the context of the end of life, and specifically in the last days.

The WHO defines quality of life "as an individual's perception of their position in life in the context of the culture and value systems in which they live and in relation to their goals, expectations, standards and concerns."[12]

Whilst there has been an explosion in the past 30 years of medical and social science research into the measurement of quality of life in terms of this broad definition, focusing largely on the health outcomes of medical interventions, for the purposes of this Report, it is reasonable to consider what constitutes 'quality of life' for dying people, and how we assess it.

The importance of why we would want to assess quality of life in a person who is at the end of life, is that clinical decisions about initiating or withdrawing medical treatments or life-supporting measures often revolve around the impact that it is perceived these could have on the dying person's quality of life.

In the landmark case at the Supreme Court of *Aintree University Hospitals NHS Foundation Trust v James* (2013), Baroness Hale's summing up included:

'I also respectfully disagree with the statement that "no prospect of recovery" means "no prospect of recovering such a state of good health as will avert the looming prospect of death if the life-sustaining treatment is given". At least on the evidence before the judge, this was not, as Sir Alan Ward put it, a situation in which the patient was "actively dying". It was accepted in Burke (as it had been earlier) that where the patient is close to death, the object may properly be to make his dying as comfortable and as dignified as possible, rather than to take invasive steps to prolong his life for a short while (see paras 62-63). But where a patient is suffering from an incurable illness, disease or disability, it is not very helpful to talk of recovering a state of "good health". The patient's life may still be very well worth living. Resuming a quality of life which the patient would regard as worthwhile is more readily applicable, particularly in the case of a patient with permanent disabilities. As was emphasised in Re J (1991), it is not for others to say that a life which the patient would regard as worthwhile is not worth living.' [13]

We must consider not only the condition of a person who is 'actively dying', but also a person with 'an incurable illness, disease or disability' that could lead to death. We hold it to be a self-evident truth that only the person who is in either of those situations can offer the definitive assessment of what their present quality of life is, and whether that life is worthwhile. It is not for clinicians, who may indeed believe they have the 'best interests' of the person at heart, to make that assessment of the quality of life that is being experienced, or of the worthwhileness of that life. Ordinarily, doctors and nurses are simply not qualified to make judgments about the quality or worth of a patient's life. That is a matter for the patient themselves. That is also broadly what the law states, not only as we saw in *Aintree* by Baroness Hale, but also by Articles 8 and 9 of the European Convention and schedule 1 of the Human Rights Act 1998.

If the person who is at the end of life is unable to voice their personal opinion, because of physical or mental constraints, lack of capacity or being unconscious, the onus is on the clinicians to consult with an appointed IMCA, or someone who holds a welfare lasting power of attorney, or other family members, or to hold a 'best interests' meeting in accordance with the Mental Capacity Act 2005.

In case study 2, the Supreme Court judgement in *Aintree* was publicly discussed, but elsewhere in this Report there are either explicit examples of clinicians making unilateral judgements about a person's quality of life (see case study 3), or implying that the life of the person may not be worthwhile (see case study 4).

Recognising dying and assessing prognosis

One of the criticisms of the LCP was that junior and inexperienced staff – often with limited access to senior cover overnight and at weekends – were left to make the decision that a person was in the last days of life. Moreover, once a patient was placed on the LCP, the experience of many relatives was that it was hard to have this decision reversed. In response to this concern, NICE guideline NG31 made clear recommendations about the need to recognise dying, using a range of clinical signs to "monitor for further changes in the person at least every 24 hours and update the person's care plan"; and to "seek advice from colleagues with more experience of providing end of life care when there is a high level of uncertainty".

Furthermore, NICE guideline NG31 emphasised the need to communicate with the patient and family about these decisions; to discuss prognosis with them if they desire it; to seek out the dying person's prior wishes (e.g. in the form of an Advance Care Plan); and to recognise the role of family members with lasting power of attorney.

[Case studies 3, 6, 7, 8, 10, 16]

[1] *Bolam v Friern Hospital Management Committee* [1957] 1 WLR 582.

[2] *Bolitho v City and Hackney Health Authority* [1998] AC 232.

[3] https://www.guysandstthomas.nhs.uk/health-information/amber-care-bundle

[4] https://www.goldstandardsframework.org.uk/patients-amp-carers

[5] [2013] UKSC 67, [2014] AC 591.

[6] *Ibid,* para *43.*

[7] https://www.nhs.uk/conditions/social-care-and-support-guide/making-decisions-for-someone-else/mental-capacity-act/

[8] https://cks.nice.org.uk/topics/delirium/diagnosis/assessment/

[9] See also *An NHS Trust v Y* [2018] UKSC 46, [2019] AC 978, [2018] 3 WLR 751, [2019] 1 All ER 95.

[10] [1957] Crim LR 365.

[11] [1908] KB 454, 1 Cr App Rep 13.

[12] https://www.who.int/tools/whoqol

[13] http://www.bailii.org/uk/cases/UKSC/2013/67.html (see para. 44).

Bibliography

Care Quality Commission (CQC). (2017) A different ending. Addressing inequalities in end of life care. Overview report. https://www.cqc.org.uk/ publications/themed-work/different-ending-end-life-care-review (last accessed 1 May 2022)

Care Quality Commission (CQC). (2020) Review of Do Not Attempt Cardiopulmonary Resuscitation decisions during the COVID-19 pandemic: interim report. https://www.cqc.org.uk/publications/themed-work/review-do-not-attempt-cardiopulmonary-resuscitation-decisions-during-covid (last accessed 6 September 2022)

Economist Intelligence Unit. 2015. The 2015 Quality of Death Index: Ranking palliative care across the world. https://impact.economist.com/ perspectives/sites/default/files/ 2015%20EIU%20Quality%20of%20Death%20Index%20Oct%2029%20FINAL. pdf (last accessed 25 May 2022)

General Medical Council (GMC). (2010) Treatment and care towards the end of life: good practice in decision making. (Updated in 2022.) https:// www.gmc-uk.org/ethical-guidance/ethical-guidance-for-doctors/treatment-and-care-towards-the-end-of-life (last accessed 27 May 2022)

Hawkes CA, Fritz Z, Deas G, Ahmedzai SH et al. (2020) Development of the Recommended Summary Plan for Emergency Care and Treatment (ReSPECT). *Resuscitation*. Mar 1;148:98-107.

House of Lords. Health and Care Act 2022, Lord Kamall's amendment, Clause 16(6). https://bills.parliament.uk/bills/3022/stages/16122/ amendments/91465 (last accessed 27 May 2022)

Leadership Alliance for the Care of Dying People. (2014). One chance to get it right. (2014) Department of Health and Social Care. https://www.gov.uk/ government/news/new-approach-to-care-for-the-dying-published (last accessed 20 May 2022)

Mental Capacity Act 2005. https://www.legislation.gov.uk/ukpga/2005/9/ contents (last accessed 10 October 2022)

Liverpool Care Pathway (LCP) Review Panel. (2013) More Care, Less Pathway. https://assets.publishing.service.gov.uk/government/uploads/system/uploads/attachment_data/file/212450/Liverpool_Care_Pathway.pdf (last accessed 27 May 2022)

NHS. Palliative and end of life care. https://www.england.nhs.uk/eolc/ (last accessed 28 April 2022)

NHS. Palliative and End of Life Care. Statutory Guidance for Integrated Care Boards (ICBs) (2022) https://www.england.nhs.uk/publication/palliative-and-end-of-life-care-statutory-guidance-for-integrated-care-boards-icbs/ (last accessed 06 September 2022)

National Audit of Care at the End of Life (NACEL). (2022) NACEL round 3 report. https://www.nhsbenchmarking.nhs.uk/news/nacel-round-three-reports-now-published (last accessed 7 October 2022)

National Institute for Health and Care Excellence (NICE). (2012, last updated 2016) Palliative care for adults: strong opioids for pain relief. https://www.nice.org.uk/Guidance/CG140 (last accessed 03 October 2022)

National Institute for Health and Care Excellence (NICE) (2015) Care of dying adults in the last days of life. (NG31) https://www.nice.org.uk/guidance/ng31 (last accessed 26 May 2022)

National Institute for Health and Care Excellence (NICE) (2017) Care of dying adults in the last days of life. Quality standard [QS144] https://www.nice.org.uk/guidance/qs144 (last accessed 26 January 2023)

National Institute for Health and Care Excellence (NICE). (2020) NICE impact: end of life care for adults. https://www.nice.org.uk/about/what-we-do/into-practice/measuring-the-use-of-nice-guidance/impact-of-our-guidance/nice-impact-end-of-life-care-for-adults (last accessed 27 May 2022)

Wiffen PJ, Derry S, Moore RA. (2014) Impact of morphine, fentanyl, oxycodone or codeine on patient consciousness, appetite and thirst when used to treat cancer pain. *Cochrane Database of Systematic Reviews* 2014, Issue 5. Art. No.: CD011056.

World Health Organisation. 1987 (updated). Definition of 'palliative care'. https://www.who.int/news-room/fact-sheets/detail/palliative-care (last accessed 29 April 2022)

Appendices

Appendix 1

Selection of 44 recommendations from More Care, Less Pathway, LCP Review Panel (2013)

Appendix 2

Five priorities for care. From: One Chance to Get it Right (2014)

Appendix 3

NICE Guideline NG31 on End of Life Care for Adults in Last Days of Life (2015), selected recommendations

Appendix 4

GMC Guidance on End of Life Care (2010, updated 2022), selected extracts

Appendix 5

Coroner's and Justice Act, ss1, 4, 6 (2009)

Appendix 6

The Notification of Deaths Regulations (2019)

Appendix 7

Lessons from the failure of an attempt to improve the experience of dying in acute hospitals. Extract from Lancet Commission on Value of Death (2022)

Appendix 8

ReSPECT process. Abstract of first publication by Hawkes et al (2020) and latest version of ReSPECT form (4 pages)

Appendix 9

NHS Health and Care Act 2022 and Guidance on palliative care for Integrated Care Boards (2022)

Appendix 1

Selected recommendations from Neuberger LCP Review panel, with relevance to this Report.

Source: More Care, Less Pathway (2013)

In this table, we have selected recommendations from the Neuberger LCP Review panel report, and linked them to case studies where these recommendations may be relevant. We also link the recommendations to the Calls for Remedial Action that we propose.

Key: 'Rec.' refers to number of recommendation in 'More Care, Less Pathway'

Rec.	Theme	More Care, Less Pathway Recommendation	Relevance to case studies	Relevance to 'Call for remedial actions'
3	Terminology	The name 'Liverpool Care Pathway' should be abandoned, and within the area of end of life care, the term 'pathway' should be avoided. An 'end of life care plan' should be sufficient for both professionals and lay people.	1, 2, 3, 5, 6, 7, 9, 10, 11, 12, 15, 16	1
4	Evidence base – Patient experience	The CQC and the Health Quality Improvement Partnership, should conduct fully independent assessments of the role of healthcare professionals in end of life care in England, focusing on the outcomes and experience of care, as reported by patients, their relatives and carers, as well as the quality of dying.	All cases	2, 3, 4, 5, 6

7	Falsification of documentation	Clinicians should be reminded by their registration bodies that the deliberate falsification of any document or clinical record, in order to deflect future criticism of a failure of care, is contrary to GMC and NMC guidelines and therefore a disciplinary matter.	3	2, 3, 4
8	Diagnosis of dying – prognostic tools	NHS England and Health Education England should collaborate to promote: • the use of evidence-based prognostic tools, including awareness of their limitations; and • evidence-based education and competency based training, with regular refresher modules, for all professionals working with people approaching the end of their lives, both in the use of prognostic tools and in explanation to patients and relatives or carers of how they are used and the unavoidable uncertainties that accompany an individual's dying.	All cases	1, 6
11	Diagnosis of dying- communicating uncertainty	The National Institute for Health Research should as a matter of priority fund research into the development and evaluation of education and training methods and programmes addressing uncertainty and communication when caring for the dying.	3, 6, 7, 8, 10, 14, 16	2, 3, 4
14	Decisions to initiate end of life care plan out of hours	Every patient diagnosed as dying should have a clearly identified senior responsible clinician accountable for their care during any 'out of hours' period. Unless it is unavoidable, urgent, and is clearly in the patient's best interests, the decision to withdraw or not to start a life-	All cases	2, 3, 4, 5

		prolonging treatment should be taken in the cool light of day by the senior responsible clinician in consultation with the healthcare team. The practice of making such decisions in the middle of the night, at weekends or on Bank Holidays, by staff that do not have the requisite training and competence, should cease forthwith.		
16	Training in shared decision making	The Review panel is deeply concerned that the GMC guidance is clearly not always being followed in the care of the dying, and recommends that the Royal Colleges review the effectiveness of any training in shared decision-making that they provide, examining the extent to which it closely reflects the professional standards in GMC and NMC guidance and required competencies in this area, with a view to ensuring continued competence is maintained across the education and training spectrum from undergraduate teaching and learning through to continued professional development.	2, 5, 7, 8, 10, 11, 14, 15	2, 3, 4, 5
17, 18, 19, 20, 21, 22	Nutrition and Hydration	17. The GMC should review its guidance on supporting oral nutrition and hydration to consider whether stronger emphasis should be given to this issue. 18. The Nursing and Midwifery Council should urgently produce guidance for nurses on supporting oral nutrition and hydration. 19. All staff in contact with patients should be trained in the appropriate use of hydration and nutrition at the end of life and how to discuss this with patients, their relatives and carers.	4, 5, 6, 7, 8, 9, 10, 11, 15, 16	2, 3, 4, 5, 6

		Recommendation		
		20. There should be a duty on all staff to ensure that patients who are able to eat and drink should be supported to do so. 21. Failure to support oral hydration and nutrition when still possible and desired should be regarded as professional misconduct. 22. Specialist services, professional associations and the Royal Colleges should run and evaluate programmes of education, training and audit about how to discuss and decide with patients and relatives or carers how to manage hydration at the end of life.		
23, 24	Sedation and Pain Relief	23. Before a syringe driver is commenced this must be discussed as far as possible with the patient, their relatives or carers, and the reasoning documented. 24. New research is needed on the use of drugs at end of life, and in particular on the extent to which sedative and analgesic drugs themselves contribute to reduced consciousness, and perceived reduction of appetite and thirst.	1, 3, 5, 6, 12, 13, 15	2, 3, 4, 5, 6
29, 30	Documenting an end of life care plan and communication	29. Guidance should specify that the senior clinician writes in the patient's notes a record of the face to face conversation in which the end of life care plan was first discussed with the patient's relatives or carers. The record of that conversation must include the following: • That the clinician explained that the patient is now dying and when and how death might be expected to occur.	10, 14, 16	1, 2, 3, 4, 5,

		1, 2, 3, 4	
	2, 7, 8, 13, 14, 15		All cases
	• If the family or carers do not accept that the patient is dying, the clinician has explained the basis for that judgement. • That the relatives or carers had the opportunity to ask questions. 30. A shared care folder, kept at the hospital bedside and designed for communication between patients, relatives and the staff, should be introduced, supported by training for staff on how to use it.	For each patient on an end of life care plan that has no means of expressing preferences and no representation by a relative or carer, views on their care should be represented by an independent advocate, whether appointed under the Mental Capacity Act 2005, a chaplain, or an appropriate person provided through a voluntary organisation. This applies to people of whatever age who lack capacity.	As part of its work to review the Nursing and Midwifery Code in preparation for revalidation, and as a matter of priority the Nursing and Midwifery Council should provide guidance for nurses caring for people at end of life. This should encompass the good practice guidance on decision-making recommended in paragraph 1.42.
	32	Independent Advocacy	34	Guidance for nurses in end of life care

Reconstructed table:

#	Topic	col A	col B
32	Independent Advocacy	2, 7, 8, 13, 14, 15	1, 2, 3, 4
34	Guidance for nurses in end of life care	All cases	1, 2, 3, 4
39	A system-wide strategic approach to	All cases	1, 4, 6

39 — A system-wide strategic approach to — The system needs a coalition of regulatory and professional bodies with NHS England, along with patient groups, setting clear expectations for a high standard of — All cases — 1, 4, 6

improving care for the dying	care for dying patients – care that will also meet the important and sometimes neglected needs of their relatives and carers. Working together strategically, such a coalition should lead the way in creating and delivering the knowledge base, the education training and skills and the long term commitment needed to make high quality care for dying patients a reality, not just an ambition. As a minimum, this would entail close co-operation between the GMC, NMC, the Royal Colleges, the CQC, NHS England and NICE. Under this approach, the GMC and NMC would take the lead with the Royal Colleges, Health Education England and NHS England in: • Providing any additional good practice guidance, building on the standards set out in the GMC guidance on treatment and care towards the end of life • Reviewing whether current education and training standards adequately address care of the dying; setting requirements based on agreed levels of competence in the care of dying patients; and quality assuring the outcomes and effectiveness of teaching and learning. • Setting relevant standards for continuing professional development, for all clinicians (generalist and specialists) who have a role in caring for dying patients and their relatives or carers. And, where appropriate, encouraging or facilitating the development of

	relevant resources or programmes for continuing professional development. • As part of this coalition, the CQC would collaborate with patient groups in defining what good quality end of life care services should look like and then inspect against those standards.	
41	Thematic review of end of life care	The CQC should carry out a thematic review within the next 12 months of how dying patients are treated across the various settings, from acute hospitals to nursing and care homes as well as hospice and the community.	All cases	1, 4

Appendix 2

Five priorities for care
for people who are dying.

From: Leadership Alliance (2014). *One Chance to Get it Right.*

1. The possibility that a person may die within the coming days and hours is recognised and communicated clearly, decisions about care are made in accordance with the person's needs and wishes, and these are reviewed and revised regularly by doctors and nurses.

2. Sensitive communication takes place between staff and the person who is dying and those important to them.

3. The dying person, and those identified as important to them, are involved in decisions about treatment and care.

4. The people important to the dying person are listened to and their needs are respected.

5. Care is tailored to the individual and delivered with compassion – with an individual care plan in place.

Appendix 3

NICE guideline NG31 (2015).
Care of dying adults in the last days of life

Below are selected parts and recommendations of the NICE guideline NG31 which are cited in this Report. The full guideline can be found at https://www.nice.org.uk/guidance/ng31

Overview

This guideline covers the clinical care of adults (18 years and over) who are dying during the last 2 to 3 days of life. It aims to improve end of life care for people in their last days of life by communicating respectfully and involving them, and the people important to them, in decisions and by maintaining their comfort and dignity. The guideline covers how to manage common symptoms without causing unacceptable side effects and maintain hydration in the last days of life.

Who is it for?

• Health and social care professionals caring for people who are dying, including those working in primary care, care homes, hospices, hospitals and community care settings such as people's own homes

• Commissioners and providers of care for people in the last days of life

• People who are dying, their families, carers and other people important to them.

Context

Without an evidence-based approach to the care of dying people, there is a danger of placing tradition and familiar policies before the needs of individuals and families. The Liverpool Care Pathway (LCP) for the Care of the Dying Adult and its numerous local derivatives were widely adopted in the NHS and UK hospices until 2014. Although the LCP was designed to bring values of 'good' end of life care from the hospice movement to mainstream hospitals and elsewhere, it met with increasing criticism from the public, healthcare professions and the media. There were 3 main areas of concern:

• recognising that a person was dying was not always supported by an experienced clinician and not reliably reviewed, even if the person may have had potential to improve

• the dying person may have been unduly sedated as a result of injudiciously prescribed symptom control medicines

• the perception that hydration and some essential medicines may have been withheld or withdrawn, resulting in a negative effect on the dying person.

These were not necessarily a direct consequence of following the LCP, but often happened because of poor or indiscriminate implementation and a lack of staff training and supervision.

This guideline responds to a need for an evidence-based guideline for the clinical care of the dying adult throughout the NHS. It is focused on care needed when a person is judged by the multiprofessional clinical team to be within a few (2 to 3) days of death. This is different from other important NHS initiatives labelled 'end of life care' which are aimed at improving care for people in the last year or so of a chronic condition.

Although the guideline focuses on the people who are thought to be in the last few days of life, for many people, especially those in a gradual decline, the principles of communication, shared decision-making and pharmacological care can be applied far earlier in their care. The recommendations apply to all people at the end of life, whether they are conscious or unconscious.

For some people who are entering the last days of life, mental capacity to understand and engage in shared decision-making may be limited. This could be temporary or fluctuating, for example it may be caused by delirium associated with an infection or a biochemical imbalance such as dehydration or organ failure, or it could be a permanent loss of capacity from dementia or other similar irreversible conditions. The guideline complements, but does not replace the healthcare professional and other's duty to comply with the Mental Capacity Act. It also makes clear the duties of the multiprofessional team regarding communication and involving those people important to the dying person.

Recommendations

1.1 Recognising when a person may be in the last days of life

These recommendations are intended to help healthcare professionals to recognise when a person may be entering the last days of their life, or if they may be deteriorating, stabilising or improving even temporarily. It can often be difficult to be certain that a person is dying. The recommendations supplement the individual clinical judgement that is needed to make decisions about the level of certainty of prognosis and how to manage any uncertainty.

1.1.1   If it is thought that a person may be entering the last days of life, gather and document information on:

- the person's physiological, psychological, social and spiritual needs

- current clinical signs and symptoms

- medical history and the clinical context, including underlying diagnoses

- the person's goals and wishes

- the views of those important to the person about future care.

1.1.2   Assess for changes in signs and symptoms in the person and review any investigation results that have already been reported that may suggest a person is entering the last days of life. These changes include the following:

- signs such as agitation, Cheyne-Stokes breathing, deterioration in level of consciousness, mottled skin, noisy respiratory secretions and progressive weight loss

- symptoms such as increasing fatigue and loss of appetite

- functional observations such as changes in communication, deteriorating mobility or performance status, or social withdrawal.

1.1.3   Be aware that improvement in signs and symptoms or functional observations could indicate that the person may be stabilising or recovering.

1.1.4 Avoid undertaking investigations that are unlikely to affect care in the last few days of life unless there is a clinical need to do so, for example, when a blood count could guide the use of platelet transfusion to avoid catastrophic bleeding.

1.1.5 Use the knowledge gained from the assessments and other information gathered from the multiprofessional team, the person and those important to them, to help determine whether the person is nearing death, deteriorating, stable or improving.

1.1.6 Monitor for further changes in the person at least every 24 hours and update the person's care plan.

1.1.7 Seek advice from colleagues with more experience of providing end of life care when there is a high level of uncertainty (for example, ambiguous or conflicting clinical signs or symptoms) about whether a person is entering the last days of life, may be stabilising or if there is potential for even temporary recovery.

1.2 Communication

Please also refer to the recommendations on communication in *NICE's guideline on patient experience in adult NHS services.*

Healthcare professionals caring for adults at the end of life need to take into consideration the person's current mental capacity to communicate and actively participate in their end of life care (for more information see *NICE's information on making decisions about your care*).

1.2.1 Establish the communication needs and expectations of people who may be entering their last days of life, taking into account:

- if they would like a person important to them to be present when making decisions about their care

- their current level of understanding that they may be nearing death

- their cognitive status and if they have any specific speech, language or other communication needs

- how much information they would like to have about their prognosis

- any cultural, religious, social or spiritual needs or preferences.

1.2.2 Discuss the dying person's prognosis with them (unless they do not wish to be informed) as soon as it is recognised that they may be entering the last days of life and include those important to them in the discussion if the dying person wishes.

1.2.3 Provide the dying person, and those important to them, with:

- accurate information about their prognosis (unless they do not wish to be informed), explaining any uncertainty and how this will be managed, but avoiding false optimism

- an opportunity to talk about any fears and anxieties, and to ask questions about their care in the last days of life accurate information about their prognosis (unless they do not wish to be informed), explaining any uncertainty and how this will be managed, but avoiding false optimism

- information about how to contact members of their care team

- opportunities for further discussion with a member of their care team.

1.2.4 Explore with the dying person and those important to them:

- whether the dying person has an advance statement or has stated preferences about their care in the last days of life (including any anticipatory prescribing decisions or an advance decision to refuse treatment or details of any legal lasting power of attorney for health and welfare)

- whether the dying person has understood and can retain the information given about their prognosis.

1.2.5 Discuss the dying person's prognosis with other members of the multiprofessional care team, and ensure that this is documented in the dying person's record of care.

1.3 Shared decision-making

The recommendations in this section cover shared decision-making in the last days of life. Healthcare professionals caring for adults at the end of life need to take into consideration the person's current mental capacity to engage and actively participate in shared decision-making on their end of life care (for more information see *NICE's information on making decisions about your care*).

Please also refer to *NICE's guideline on shared decision making*.

1.3.1 Establish the level of involvement that the dying person wishes to have and is able to have in shared decision-making, and ensure that honesty and transparency are used when discussing the development and implementation of their care plan.

1.3.2 As part of any shared decision-making process take into account:

- whether the dying person has an advance statement or an advance decision to refuse treatment in place, or has provided details of any legal lasting power of attorney for health and welfare their current level of understanding that they may be nearing death

- the person's current goals and wishes

- whether the dying person has any cultural, religious, social or spiritual preferences.

1.3.3 Identify a named lead healthcare professional, who is responsible for encouraging shared decision-making in the person's last days of life. The named healthcare professional should:

- give information about how they can be contacted and contact details for relevant out-of-hours services to the dying person and those important to them their current level of understanding that they may be nearing death

- ensure that any agreed changes to the care plan are understood by the dying person, those important to them, and those involved in the dying person's care.

1.4 Maintaining hydration

1.4.1 Support the dying person to drink if they wish to and are able to. Check for any difficulties, such as swallowing problems or risk of aspiration. Discuss the risks and benefits of continuing to drink, with the dying person, and those involved in the dying person's care.

1.4.2 Offer frequent care of the mouth and lips to the dying person, and include the management of dry mouth in their care plan, if needed. Offer the person the following, as needed:

- help with cleaning their teeth or dentures, if they would like

- frequent sips of fluid.

1.4.3 Encourage people important to the dying person to help with mouth and lip care or giving drinks, if they wish to. Provide any necessary aids and give them advice on giving drinks safely.

1.4.4 Assess, preferably daily, the dying person's hydration status, and review the possible need for starting clinically assisted hydration, respecting the person's wishes and preferences.

1.4.5 Discuss the risks and benefits of clinically assisted hydration with the dying person and those important to them. Advise them that, for someone who is in the last days of life:

- clinically assisted hydration may relieve distressing symptoms or signs related to dehydration, but may cause other problems (see recommendation 1.4.9)

- it is uncertain if giving clinically assisted hydration will prolong life or extend the dying process

- it is uncertain if not giving clinically assisted hydration will hasten death.

1.4.6 Ensure that any concerns raised by the dying person or those important to them are addressed before starting clinically assisted hydration.

1.4.7 When considering clinically assisted hydration for a dying person, use an individualised approach and take into account:

- whether they have expressed a preference for or against clinically assisted hydration, or have any cultural, spiritual or religious beliefs that might affect this documented in an advance statement or an advance decision to refuse treatment

- their level of consciousness

- any swallowing difficulties

- their level of thirst
- the risk of pulmonary oedema
- whether even temporary recovery is possible.

1.4.8 Consider a therapeutic trial of clinically assisted hydration if the person has distressing symptoms or signs that could be associated with dehydration, such as thirst or delirium, and oral hydration is inadequate.

1.4.9 For people being started on clinically assisted hydration:

- Monitor at least every 12 hours for changes in the symptoms or signs of dehydration, and for any evidence of benefit or harm.
- Continue with clinically assisted hydration if there are signs of clinical benefit.
- Reduce or stop clinically assisted hydration if there are signs of possible harm to the dying person, such as fluid overload, or if they no longer want it.

1.4.10 For people already dependent on clinically assisted hydration (enteral or parenteral) before the last days of life:

- Review the risks and benefits of continuing clinically assisted hydration with the person and those important to them.
- Consider whether to continue, reduce or stop clinically assisted hydration as the person nears death.

1.5 Pharmacological interventions

Providing appropriate non-pharmacological methods of symptom management is an important part of high-quality care at the end of life, for example, re-positioning to manage pain or using fans to minimise the impact of breathlessness, but this has not been addressed in this guideline. This section focuses on the pharmacological management of common symptoms at the end of life and includes general recommendations for non-specialists prescribing medicines to manage these symptoms.

1.5.1 When it is recognised that a person may be entering the last days of life, review their current medicines and, after discussion and agreement with the dying person and those important to them (as appropriate), stop any previously prescribed medicines that are not providing symptomatic benefit or that may cause harm.

1.5.2 When involving the dying person and those important to them in making decisions about symptom control in the last days of life:

- Use the dying person's individualised care plan to help decide which medicines are clinically appropriate.

- Discuss the benefits and harms of any medicines offered.

1.5.3 When considering medicines for symptom control, take into account:

- the likely cause of the symptom

- the dying person's preferences alongside the benefits and harms of the medicine

- any individual or cultural views that might affect their choice

- any other medicines being taken to manage symptoms

- any risks of the medicine that could affect prescribing decisions, for example prescribing cyclizine to manage nausea and vomiting may exacerbate heart failure.

1.5.4 Decide on the most effective route for administering medicines in the last days of life tailored to the dying person's condition, their ability to swallow safely and their preferences.

1.5.5 Consider prescribing different routes of administering medicine if the dying person is unable to take or tolerate oral medicines. Avoid giving intramuscular injections and give either subcutaneous or intravenous injections.

1.5.6 Consider using a syringe pump to deliver medicines for continuous symptom control if more than 2 or 3 doses of any 'as required' medicines have been given within 24 hours.

1.5.7 For people starting treatment who have not previously been given medicines for symptom management, start with the lowest effective dose and titrate as clinically indicated.

1.5.8 Regularly reassess, at least daily, the dying person's symptoms during treatment to inform appropriate titration of medicine.

1.5.9 Seek specialist palliative care advice if the dying person's symptoms do not improve promptly with treatment or if there are undesirable side effects, such as unwanted sedation.

[Detailed recommendations on managing individual symptoms pharmacologically are omitted here]

1.6 Anticipatory prescribing

1.6.1 Use an individualised approach to prescribing anticipatory medicines for people who are likely to need symptom control in the last days of life. Specify the indications for use and the dosage of any medicines prescribed.

1.6.2 Assess what medicines the person might need to manage symptoms likely to occur during their last days of life (such as agitation, anxiety, breathlessness, nausea and vomiting, noisy respiratory secretions and pain). Discuss any prescribing needs with the dying person, those important to them and the multiprofessional team.

1.6.3 Ensure that suitable anticipatory medicines and routes are prescribed as early as possible. Review these medicines as the dying person's needs change.

1.6.4 When deciding which anticipatory medicines to offer take into account:

- the likelihood of specific symptoms occurring
- the benefits and harms of prescribing or administering medicines
- the benefits and harms of not prescribing or administering medicines
- the possible risk of the person suddenly deteriorating (for example, catastrophic haemorrhage or seizures) for which urgent symptom control may be needed
- the place of care and the time it would take to obtain medicines.

1.6.5 Before anticipatory medicines are administered, review the dying person's individual symptoms and adjust the individualised care plan and prescriptions as necessary.

1.6.6 If anticipatory medicines are administered:

- Monitor for benefits and any side effects at least daily, and give feedback to the lead healthcare professional.
- Adjust the individualised care plan and prescription as necessary.

Appendix 4

General Medical Council
Treatment and care towards the end of life: good practice in decision making.

First published 20 May 2010, updated 15 March 2022.
Below are **extracts** from the GMC document.

Guidance

1. Patients who are approaching the end of their life need high-quality treatment and care that support them to live as well as possible until they die, and to die with dignity. This guidance identifies a number of challenges in ensuring that patients receive such care, and provides a framework to support you in addressing the issues in a way that meets the needs of individual patients. Providing treatment and care towards the end of life will often involve decisions that are clinically complex and emotionally distressing; and some decisions may involve ethical dilemmas and uncertainties about the law that further complicate the decision-making process. This guidance is intended to help you, in whatever context you are working, to address these issues effectively with patients, the healthcare team and those who have an interest in the patient's welfare. It seeks to ensure that people who are close to the patient (partners, family, carers and others) are involved and supported, while the patient is receiving care and after the patient has died.

2. For the purposes of this guidance, patients are 'approaching the end of life' when they are likely to die within the next 12 months. This includes patients whose death is imminent (expected within a few hours or days) and those with:
   - advanced, progressive, incurable conditions
   - general frailty and co-existing conditions that mean they are expected to die within 12 months
   - existing conditions if they are at risk of dying from a sudden acute crisis in their condition
   - life-threatening acute conditions caused by sudden catastrophic events.

Principles

Equalities and human rights

7. You must give patients who are approaching the end of their life the same quality of care as all other patients. You must treat patients and those close to them with dignity, respect and compassion, especially when they are facing difficult situations and decisions about care. You must respect their privacy and right to confidentiality.

8. Some groups of patients can experience inequalities in getting access to healthcare services and in the standard of care provided. It is known that some older people, people with disabilities and people from ethnic minorities have received poor standards of care towards the end of life. This can be because of physical, communication and other barriers, and mistaken beliefs or lack of knowledge among those providing services, about the patient's needs and interests. Equalities, capacity and human rights laws reinforce your ethical duty to treat patients fairly.

9. If you are involved in decisions about treatment and care towards the end of life, you must be aware of the Human Rights Act 1998 and its main provisions, as your decisions are likely to engage the basic rights and principles set out in the Act.

Presumption in favour of prolonging life

10. Following established ethical and legal (including human rights) principles, decisions concerning potentially life-prolonging treatment must not be motivated by a desire to bring about the patient's death, and must start from a presumption in favour of prolonging life. This presumption will normally require you to take all reasonable steps to prolong a patient's life. However, there is no absolute obligation to prolong life irrespective of the consequences for the patient, and irrespective of the patient's views, if they are known or can be found out.

Presumption of capacity

11. You must work on the presumption that every adult patient has the capacity to make decisions about their care and treatment. You must not assume that a patient lacks capacity to make a decision solely because of their age, disability, appearance, behaviour, medical

condition (including mental illness), beliefs, apparent inability to communicate or because they make a decision that others disagree with or consider unwise.

Maximising capacity to make decisions

12. If a patient's capacity to make a decision may be impaired, you must provide the patient with all appropriate help and support to maximise their ability to understand, retain, use or weigh up the information needed to make that decision or communicate their wishes. You must assess their capacity to make each decision, at the time it needs to be made. You can find detailed guidance about maximising and assessing a patient's capacity in *Decision making and consent* and in the codes of practice supporting the *Mental Capacity Act 2005* and *Adults with Incapacity (Scotland) Act 2000.*

Overall benefit

13. If an adult patient lacks capacity to decide, the decisions you or others make on the patient's behalf must be based on whether treatment would be of overall benefit to the patient (see paragraphs 40–46 for more about assessing overall benefit). When you are responsible for making the decision about overall benefit, you must consult with those close to the patient who lacks capacity, to help you reach a view (see paragraphs 15–16).

Meeting patients' nutrition and hydration needs

109. All patients are entitled to food and drink of adequate quantity and quality and to the help they need to eat and drink. Malnutrition and dehydration can be both a cause and consequence of ill health, so maintaining a healthy level of nutrition and hydration can help to prevent or treat illness and symptoms and improve treatment outcomes for patients. You must keep the nutrition and hydration status of your patients under review. You should be satisfied that nutrition and hydration are being provided in a way that meets your patients' needs, and that if necessary patients are being given adequate help to enable them to eat and drink.

110. If a patient refuses food or drink or has problems eating or drinking,

you should first assess and address any underlying physical or psychological causes that could be improved with treatment or care. For example, some patients stop eating because of depression, or pain caused by mouth ulcers or dentures, or for other reasons that can be addressed. If a patient needs assistance in eating or drinking that is not being provided, or if underlying problems are not being effectively managed, you should take steps to rectify the situation, if you can. If you cannot, you should inform an appropriate person within the organisation that is responsible for the patient's care.

111. If you are concerned that a patient is not receiving adequate nutrition or hydration by mouth, even with support, you must carry out an assessment of their condition and their individual requirements. You must assess their needs for nutrition and hydration separately and consider what forms of clinically assisted nutrition or hydration may be required to meet their needs.

Clinically assisted nutrition and hydration

112. Clinically assisted nutrition includes intravenous feeding, and feeding by nasogastric tube and by percutaneous endoscopic gastrostomy (PEG) and radiologically inserted gastrostomy (RIG) feeding tubes through the abdominal wall. All these means of providing nutrition also provide fluids necessary to keep patients hydrated. Clinically assisted hydration can also be provided by intravenous or subcutaneous infusion of fluids through a 'drip'. The terms 'clinically assisted nutrition' and 'clinically assisted hydration' do not refer to help given to patients to eat or drink, for example by spoon feeding.

113. Providing nutrition and hydration by tube or drip may provide symptom relief, or prolong or improve the quality of the patient's life; but they may also present problems. The current evidence about the benefits, burdens and risks of these techniques as patients approach the end of life is not clear-cut. This can lead to concerns that patients who are unconscious or semi-conscious may be experiencing distressing symptoms and complications, or otherwise be suffering either because their needs for nutrition or hydration are not being met or because attempts to meet their perceived needs for nutrition or hydration may be causing them avoidable suffering.

114. Nutrition and hydration provided by tube or drip are regarded in law as medical treatment, and should be treated in the same way as other medical interventions. Nonetheless, some people see nutrition and hydration, whether taken orally or by tube or drip, as part of basic nurture for the patient that should almost always be provided. For this reason it is especially important that you listen to and consider the views of the patient and of those close to them (including their cultural and religious views) and explain the issues to be considered, including the benefits, burdens and risks of providing clinically assisted nutrition and hydration. You should make sure that patients, those close to them and the healthcare team understand that, when clinically assisted nutrition or hydration would be of overall benefit, it will always be offered; and that if a decision is taken not to provide clinically assisted nutrition or hydration, the patient will continue to receive high-quality care, with any symptoms addressed.

115. If disagreement arises between you and the patient (or those close to a patient who lacks capacity), or you and other members of the healthcare team, or between the team and those close to the patient, about whether clinically assisted nutrition or hydration should be provided, you should seek resolution following the guidance in paragraphs 47–49. You should make sure that the patient, or someone acting on their behalf, is informed and given advice on the patient's rights and how to access their own legal advice or representation.

Patients who have capacity

116. If you consider that a patient is not receiving adequate nutrition or hydration by mouth, you should follow the decision model in paragraph 14. You must assess the patient's nutrition and hydration needs separately and offer the patient those treatments you consider to be clinically appropriate because, for example, they would provide symptom relief or would be likely to prolong the patient's life. You must explain to the patient the benefits, burdens and risks associated with the treatments, so that the patient can make a decision about whether to accept them.

117. If you assess that clinically assisted nutrition or hydration would not be clinically appropriate, you must monitor the patient's condition and

reassess the benefits, burdens and risks of providing clinically assisted nutrition or hydration as the patient's condition changes. If a patient asks you to provide nutrition or hydration by tube or drip, you should discuss the issues with the patient and explore the reasons for their request. You must reassess the benefits, burdens and risks of providing the treatment requested, giving weight to the patient's wishes and values. When the benefits, burdens and risks are finely balanced, the patient's request will usually be the deciding factor. However, if after discussion you still consider that the treatment would not be clinically appropriate, you do not have to provide it. But you should explain your reasons to the patient and explain any other options that are available, including the option to seek a second opinion.

118. If a patient lacks capacity and cannot eat or drink enough to meet their nutrition or hydration needs, you must assess whether providing clinically assisted nutrition or hydration would be of overall benefit to them, following the decision model in paragraph 16 and guidance in paragraphs 40–48. Clinically assisted nutrition or hydration will usually be of overall benefit if, for example, they prolong life or provide symptom relief. You must assess the patient's nutrition and hydration needs separately. You must monitor the patient's condition, and reassess the benefits, burdens and risks of providing clinically assisted nutrition or hydration as the patient's condition changes.

Incapacitated adults: not expected to die in hours or days

119. If a patient is in the end stage of a disease or condition, but you judge that their death is not expected within hours or days, you must provide clinically assisted nutrition or hydration if it would be of overall benefit to them, taking into account the patient's beliefs and values, any previous request for nutrition or hydration by tube or drip and any other views they previously expressed about their care. The patient's request must be given weight and, when the benefits, burdens and risks are finely balanced, will usually be the deciding factor.

120. You must assess the patient's nutrition and hydration needs separately. If you judge that the provision of clinically assisted nutrition or hydration would not be of overall benefit to the patient, you may conclude that the treatment should not be started at that time or

should be withdrawn. You should explain your view to the patient, if appropriate, and those close to them, and respond to any questions or concerns they express.

121. In these circumstances you must make sure that the patient's interests have been thoroughly considered. This means you must take all reasonable steps to get a second opinion from a senior clinician (who might be from another discipline) who has experience of the patient's condition but who is not already directly involved in the patient's care. This opinion should be based on an examination of the patient by the clinician. In exceptional circumstances, if this is not possible for practical reasons, you must still get advice from a colleague, for example by telephone, having given them up-to-date information about the patient's condition. You should also consider seeking legal advice.

122. If you reach a consensus that clinically assisted nutrition or hydration would not be of overall benefit to the patient and the treatment is withdrawn or not started, you must make sure that the patient is kept comfortable and that any distressing symptoms are addressed. You must monitor the patient's condition and be prepared to reassess the benefits, burdens and risks of providing clinically assisted nutrition or hydration in light of changes in their condition. If clinically assisted nutrition or hydration is started or reinstated after a later assessment, and you subsequently conclude that it would not be of overall benefit to continue with the treatment, you must seek a second opinion (or, if this is not possible, seek advice), following the advice in paragraph 121.

Incapacitated adults: expected to die in hours or days

123. If a patient is expected to die within hours or days, and you consider that the burdens or risks of providing clinically assisted nutrition or hydration outweigh the benefits they are likely to bring, it will not usually be appropriate to start or continue treatment. You must consider the patient's needs for nutrition and hydration separately.

124. If a patient has previously requested that nutrition or hydration be provided until their death, or those close to the patient are sure that this is what the patient wanted, the patient's wishes must be given weight and, when the benefits, burdens and risks are finely balanced, will usually be the deciding factor.

125. You must keep the patient's condition under review, especially if they live longer than you expected. If this is the case, you must reassess the benefits, burdens and risks of providing clinically assisted nutrition or hydration, as the patient's condition changes.

Cardiopulmonary resuscitation (CPR)

128. When a person has a cardiac or respiratory arrest, CPR can be used in an attempt to restart their heart and breathing and restore their circulation. CPR is invasive, involving chest compressions, delivery of electric shocks from a defibrillator, injection of drugs, and ventilation of the lungs. If delivered promptly, CPR has a good success rate in some circumstances. Generally, however, CPR has a very low success rate and the burdens and risks of CPR include damage to internal organs and rib fractures, and adverse clinical outcomes for the patient such as hypoxic brain damage or increased physical disability. If CPR is not successful in restarting the heart or breathing, and in restoring circulation, it may mean that the patient dies in an undignified and traumatic manner.

When to consider making a Do Not Attempt CPR (DNACPR) decision

129. If cardiac or respiratory arrest is an expected part of the dying process and CPR will not be successful in restarting breathing and circulation, discussing, making and recording a decision in advance not to attempt CPR can help to ensure that the patient dies in a dignified and peaceful manner. It may also help the patient achieve their wish of spending their last hours or days at their preferred place of death. These management plans are called Do Not Attempt CPR (DNACPR) decisions and are best made in the wider context of advance care planning (see paragraphs 50–55 and glossary). A recorded DNACPR decision is not, in itself, legally binding and should be regarded as a clinical assessment and decision, made and recorded in advance, to guide immediate clinical decision-making in the event of a patient's cardiorespiratory arrest.

130. In cases in which CPR might be successful in restarting breathing and circulation, it might still not be seen as clinically appropriate because of the potential for poor clinical outcomes. When considering whether to

attempt CPR, you should consider the benefits, burdens and risks of treatment that the patient may need if CPR results in the return of a spontaneous circulation. In cases where you assess that such treatment is unlikely to be clinically appropriate, you may conclude that CPR should not be attempted. Some patients with capacity to make their own decisions may wish to refuse CPR; or in the case of patients who lack capacity it may be judged that attempting CPR would not be of overall benefit to them. However, at the time they suffer a cardiac or respiratory arrest and an immediate decision has to be made, it can be difficult to establish the patient's wishes and preferences or to get relevant information about their underlying condition to enable a fully informed assessment. So, if a patient has an existing condition that makes cardiac or respiratory arrest likely, establishing a management plan in advance will help to ensure that the patient's wishes and preferences about treatment can be taken into account and that, if appropriate, a DNACPR decision is made and recorded.

131. If a patient is admitted to hospital acutely unwell or becomes clinically unstable in their home or other place of care, and they are at foreseeable risk of cardiac or respiratory arrest, a judgement about the likely success of CPR in restarting breathing and circulation and its benefits, burdens and risks should be made as early as possible. You should also check whether any form of advance care planning is already in place and, if the patient lacks capacity, whether they have a legally binding advance refusal.

Discussions about whether to attempt CPR

Patients who have capacity

132. As with other treatments, decisions made in advance about whether CPR should be attempted must be based on the circumstances of the individual patient and take into account their wishes and preferences. It should also involve discussions with members of the healthcare team as well as (with the patient's agreement) those close to the patient. You must approach discussions sensitively and bear in mind that some patients or those close to them, may have concerns that decisions not to attempt CPR might be influenced by poorly informed or unfounded

assumptions about the impact of disability or advanced age on the patient's quality of life.

Patients who lack capacity

133. If a patient lacks capacity to make a decision about future CPR, you must consult those close to the patient as part of the decision making process. You must approach discussions sensitively and bear in mind that some people may have concerns that some decisions not to attempt CPR might be influenced by poorly informed or unfounded assumptions about the impact of disability or advanced age on the patient's quality of life. In addition, the views of members of the healthcare team involved in their care may be valuable in assessing the likelihood that CPR would be successful in restoring the patient's breathing and circulation or whether successful CPR would likely be of overall benefit to them. You must make reasonable efforts to discuss a patient's CPR status with these healthcare professionals.

When CPR will not be successful in restarting breathing and circulation

134. If a patient is at foreseeable risk of cardiac or respiratory arrest and you judge that CPR should not be attempted, because it will not be successful in restarting the patient's heart and breathing and restoring circulation, you must sensitively discuss this with the patient unless this would cause them serious harm. In this context, 'serious harm' means more than that the patient might become upset. The purpose of the dialogue is to reach a shared understanding with the patient about their situation, your judgement and your reasons for reaching it. You must listen to the patient and you should encourage them to ask questions. As part of these discussions, you should explore with the patient the type of information they want or need, their wishes or fears and explain that they have a right to seek a second opinion. While some patients may want to have these discussions, others may not. You should not force a discussion or information onto the patient if they do not want it. You should not withhold information simply because conveying it is difficult or uncomfortable for you or the healthcare team.

135. If the patient does not wish to know about or discuss a DNACPR decision, you should seek their agreement to share with those close to them, with carers and with others, the necessary information they may need to know in order to support the patient's treatment and care. You should emphasise to the patient that they may discuss the topic at any time if they decide that they want to.

136. If a patient lacks capacity, you must consult with any legal proxy and others close to the patient about the DNACPR decision and the reasons for it unless it is not practicable or appropriate to do so. These discussions should take place at the earliest practicable opportunity and should include a sensitive and careful explanation that the intention is to spare the patient treatment that will be of no benefit, not to withhold any other care or treatment the patient will need.

When CPR may be successful in restarting breathing and circulation

Patients who have capacity

137. If CPR may be successful in restarting a patient's heart and breathing and restoring circulation, the benefits must be weighed against the potential burdens and risks. This is not solely a clinical decision. You must offer the patient opportunities to discuss (with support if they need it) whether CPR should be attempted in the event of a future cardiac or respiratory arrest. You must approach this sensitively and should not force a discussion or information onto the patient if they do not want it. However, if they are prepared to talk about it, you must provide them with accurate information about the burdens and risks of CPR, including the likely clinical and other outcomes if CPR does restore breathing and circulation. This should include a sensitive explanation of the extent to which other intensive treatments and procedures may not be seen as clinically appropriate after the return of spontaneous circulation. For example, in some cases, prolonged support for multi-organ failure in an intensive care unit may not be clinically appropriate or of overall benefit even though the patient's heart has been restarted.

138. If a patient wishes to receive CPR and it is your considered judgement that CPR would not be clinically appropriate for the patient, you must sensitively explore their reasons for requesting it, their understanding of what it would involve, and their expectations about the likely outcome. As part of this, you should make sure that they have accurate information about the nature of CPR and, for example, the length of survival and level of recovery that they might realistically expect if they were successfully resuscitated. You should also try to reach agreement; for example, limited CPR interventions could be agreed in some cases. When the benefits, burdens and risks are finely balanced, the patient's request will usually be the deciding factor. If, after discussion, you still consider that CPR would not be clinically appropriate, there is no obligation to provide it in the circumstances envisaged. You must explain your reasons and any other options that may be available to the patient, including their right to seek seeking a second opinion.

Patients who lack capacity

139. If a patient lacks capacity to make a decision about future CPR, you must consult any legal proxy who has authority to make the decision for the patient unless it is not practicable or appropriate to do so. If there is no legal proxy with relevant authority, you must discuss the issue with those close to the patient and with the healthcare team. You must make all reasonable efforts to have these consultations or discussions at the earliest practicable opportunity and they should be approached with sensitivity.

In your consultations or discussions, you must follow the decision-making model in paragraph 16. In particular, you should be clear about the role that others are being asked to take in the decision-making process. If they do not have legal authority to make the decision, you should be clear that their role is to advise you and the healthcare team about the patient's wishes and preferences to inform the decision about whether attempting CPR would be of overall benefit to the patient. You must not give them the impression that it is their responsibility to decide whether CPR will be of overall benefit to the patient, or that they are being asked to decide whether or not CPR will be attempted. You should provide any legal proxy and those close to the patient, with the same information about the nature of CPR and the burdens and risks for the patient as explained in paragraph 137.

140. If the legal proxy requests that CPR is attempted in future, in spite of the burdens and risks, or they are sure that this is what the patient would want, and it is your considered judgement that CPR would not be clinically appropriate for the patient, you must sensitively explore the reasons for the proxy's request, their understanding of what it would involve, and their expectations about the likely outcome. If after further discussion you still consider that attempting CPR would not be clinically appropriate for the patient, there is no obligation to provide it in the circumstances envisaged. You should explain your reasons and any other options that may be available to the legal proxy, including their right to seek a second opinion.

Resolving disagreements

141. If there is disagreement about whether CPR should be provided, you should try to resolve it by following the guidance in paragraphs 47–49.

Resolving disagreements

47. You should aim to reach a consensus about what treatment and care would be of overall benefit to a patient who lacks capacity. Disagreements may arise between you and those close to the patient, or between you and members of the healthcare team, or between the healthcare team and those close to the patient. Depending on the seriousness of any disagreement, it is usually possible to resolve it; for example, by involving an independent advocate, seeking advice from a more experienced colleague, obtaining a second opinion, holding a case conference, or using local mediation services. In working towards a consensus, you should take into account the different decision-making roles and authority of those you consult, and the legal framework for resolving disagreements.

48. If, having taken these steps, there is still disagreement about a significant decision, you must follow any formal steps to resolve the disagreement that are required by law or set out in the relevant code of practice. You should make sure you are aware of the different

people you must consult, their different decision-making roles and the weight you must attach to their views. You should consider seeking legal advice and may need to apply to an appropriate court or statutory body for review or for an independent ruling. Your patient, those close to them and anyone appointed to act for them should be informed as early as possible of any decision to start legal proceedings, so they have the opportunity to participate or be represented.

49. In situations in which a patient with capacity to decide requests a treatment and does not accept your view that the treatment would not be clinically appropriate, the steps suggested above for resolving disagreement may also be helpful.

Appendix 5

CORONERS AND JUSTICE ACT 2009 (SECTIONS 1, 4 AND 6)

1. Duty to investigate certain deaths

(1) A senior coroner who is made aware that the body of a deceased person is within that coroner's area must as soon as practicable conduct an investigation into the person's death if subsection (2) applies.

(2) This subsection applies if the coroner has reason to suspect that—

   (a) the deceased died a violent or unnatural death,

   (b) the cause of death is unknown, or

   (c) the deceased died while in custody or otherwise in state detention.

(3) Subsection (1) is subject to sections 2 to 4.

(4) A senior coroner who has reason to believe that—

   (a) a death has occurred in or near the coroner's area,

   (b) the circumstances of the death are such that there should be an investigation into it, and

   (c) the duty to conduct an investigation into the death under subsection (1) does not arise because of the destruction, loss or absence of the body, may report the matter to the Chief Coroner.

(5) On receiving a report under subsection (4) the Chief Coroner may direct a senior coroner (who does not have to be the one who made the report) to conduct an investigation into the death.

(6) The coroner to whom a direction is given under subsection (5) must conduct an investigation into the death as soon as practicable. This is subject to section 3.

(7) A senior coroner may make whatever enquiries seem necessary in order to decide—

   (a) whether the duty under subsection (1) arises;

   (b) whether the power under subsection (4) arises.

(8) This Chapter is subject to Schedule 10.

4. Discontinuance where cause of death becomes clear before inquest

(1) A senior coroner who is responsible for conducting an investigation under this Part into a person's death must discontinue the investigation if—

(a) the coroner is satisfied that the cause of death has become clear in the course of the investigation,

(aa) an inquest into the death has not yet begun, and

(b) the coroner thinks that it is not necessary to continue the investigation.

(2) Subsection (1) does not apply if the coroner has reason to suspect that the deceased—

(a) died a violent or unnatural death, or

(b) died while in custody or otherwise in state detention.

(3) Where a senior coroner discontinues an investigation into a death under this section—

(a) the coroner may not hold an inquest into the death;

(b) no determination or finding under section 10(1) may be made in respect of the death. This subsection does not prevent a fresh investigation under this Part from being conducted into the death.

(4) A senior coroner who discontinues an investigation into a death under this section must, if requested to do so in writing by an interested person, give to that person as soon as practicable a written explanation as to why the investigation was discontinued.

6. Duty to hold inquest

A senior coroner who conducts an investigation under this Part into a person's death must (as part of the investigation) hold an inquest into the death.

This is subject to section 4(3)(a).

Appendix 6

2019 No. 1112

MEDICAL PROFESSION,
ENGLAND AND WALES CORONERS,
ENGLAND AND WALES

The Notification of Deaths Regulations 2019

[Relevant, selected **extracts** are provided below]

Citation, commencement and meaning of "relevant senior coroner"

1.—(1) These Regulations may be cited as the Notification of Deaths Regulations 2019 and come into force on 1st October 2019.

(2) In these Regulations, "relevant senior coroner" means the senior coroner appointed for the coroner area in which the body of the deceased person lies.

Duty to notify a relevant senior coroner of a death

2.—(1) A registered medical practitioner must notify the relevant senior coroner of a person's death if—

(a) the registered medical practitioner comes to know of the death on or after the coming into force of these Regulations; and

(b) at least one of the circumstances described in regulation 3(1) applies.

(2) But the duty in paragraph (1) does not apply if the registered medical practitioner reasonably believes that the relevant senior coroner has already been notified of the death under these Regulations.

Circumstances in which the duty to notify arises

3.—(1) The circumstances are—

(a) the registered medical practitioner suspects that that the person's death was due to—

(i) poisoning, including by an otherwise benign substance;

(ii) exposure to or contact with a toxic substance;

(iii) the use of a medicinal product, controlled drug or psychoactive substance;

(iv) violence;

(v) trauma or injury;

(vi) self-harm;

(vii) neglect, including self-neglect;

(viii) the person undergoing a treatment or procedure of a medical or similar nature; or

(ix) an injury or disease attributable to any employment held by the person during the person's lifetime;

(b) the registered medical practitioner suspects that the person's death was unnatural but does not fall within any of the circumstances listed in sub-paragraph (a);

(c) the registered medical practitioner—

(i) is an attending medical practitioner required to sign a certificate of cause of death in relation to the deceased person; but

(ii) despite taking reasonable steps to determine the cause of death, considers that the cause of death is unknown;

(d) the registered medical practitioner suspects that the person died while in custody or otherwise in state detention;

(e) the registered medical practitioner reasonably believes that there is no attending medical practitioner required to sign a certificate of cause of death in relation to the deceased person;

(f) the registered medical practitioner reasonably believes that—

(i) an attending medical practitioner is required to sign a certificate of cause of death in relation to the deceased person; but

(ii) the attending medical practitioner is not available within a reasonable time of the person's death to sign the certificate of cause of death;

(g) the registered medical practitioner, after taking reasonable steps to ascertain the identity of the deceased person, is unable to do so.

(2) In this regulation—

"attending medical practitioner" means a registered medical practitioner required under section 22(1) of the Births and Deaths Registration Act 1953 to sign a certificate of cause of death in relation to a deceased person;

"certificate of the cause of death" means the certificate required to be signed by a registered medical practitioner under section 22(1) of the Births and Deaths Registration Act 1953;

"controlled drug" has the same meaning as in the Misuse of Drugs Act 1971;

"employment" means any employment, whether paid or unpaid, including—

(a) work under a contract for services or as an office holder; and

(b) work experience provided pursuant to a training course or in the course of training for employment;

"medicinal product" has the same meaning given by regulation 2 of the Human Medicines Regulations 2012;

"psychoactive substance" has the same meaning as in the Psychoactive Substances Act 2016.

Notifying the relevant senior coroner

4.—(1) A registered medical practitioner who must notify a relevant senior coroner of a person's death under regulation 2(1) must do so as soon as is reasonably practicable after the duty arises.

Edward Argar
Parliamentary Under Secretary of State
Ministry of Justice

10th July 2019

Appendix 7

Lessons from the failure of an attempt to improve the experience of dying in acute hospitals

The following is an extract from: Sallnow L, Smith R, Ahmedzai SH, Bhadelia A *et al.* Report of the *Lancet* Commission on the Value of Death: bringing death back into life. *Lancet* 2022 26 February - 4 March; 399 (10327): 837–884. Reproduced with permission from Elsevier Ltd.

This section was written for the Lancet Commission Report by Baroness Rabbi Julia Neuberger and Professor Emeritus Sam H Ahmedzai.

The widespread introduction of the Liverpool Care Pathway for end-of-life care into acute hospitals in the UK (apart from Wales) was an attempt to extend palliative care beyond hospices and specialists into routine care in acute hospitals. It proved a failure but taught lessons that are broadly applicable. The pathway was first published in the late 1990s and was an integrated care pathway detailing standardised care to be delivered to dying patients and their families. It went through 12 iterations before it was published in 2013.

While anecdotal evidence suggested that the pathway helped clinicians and others provide a high-quality experience of dying within a National Health Service (NHS) setting, it was let down by three serious failings:

• First, an assumption that what worked in British hospices – institutions dedicated to care of dying people and staffed by highly skilled practitioners – could work in busy NHS hospitals with different priorities and lacking staff skilled in end-of-life care.

• Second, although the concept of an integrated pathway of care itself was acceptable, it was implemented with little or often no training, and consequently many of its actions were reduced to a "tick-box exercise" and a "one-size-fits-all solution".

• Third, despite the pathway being endorsed by national professional organisations, it severely lacked the research evidence that is expected in the adoption of any other new health technology.

Early studies did show anecdotal and qualitative evidence of benefit, but the studies did not include any controlled trials, and some had been written by the authors who had developed and promoted the pathway.

Just as the review into the pathway was being published, a formal cluster randomised controlled trial did appear, evaluating how the pathway had performed clinically in an Italian hospital setting. The trial failed to show a significant difference in the distribution of the overall quality of care toolkit scores between the wards in which the Italian version of the pathway was implemented and the control wards.

The most damning evidence, which sealed the fate of the pathway, came from the revelation that NHS hospitals were being paid to reach targets for using the pathway. This incentive contributed to the unchecked use of the pathway in hospitals and departments that had little or no training and were using it inappropriately.

After the abolition of the pathway a coalition of 21 national organisations concerned with end-of-life care declared five priorities for "care when it is thought that a person may die within the next few days or hours of life" and the UK National Institute for Health and Care Excellence (NICE) developed recommendations for clinical practice in the last days of life.

This guidance had an emphasis on individualised rather than a routine checklist approach to care of dying people.

The UK has other packages of care for looking after the dying— including the Gold Standards Framework, which is primarily intended for use in primary care, and the Amber Care Bundle. There has been little or no concern about these packages, and certainly no scandal. But none of the packages are based on the controlled trials that are expected for most interventions in health care.

We should not conclude from this story that guidelines on end-of-life care should not be attempted, but rather that they need to be based on high quality evidence, should be introduced with training and regular audit, and should not be financially incentivised. Plus, they must be used as guidance not a checklist: "Don't just read the guidance, and particularly do not just use the checklist. Engage your brains and your hearts, read and implement evidence-based guidelines, and that is what will improve care."[1]

---

[1] Neuberger J, Aaronovitch D, Bonser T, Charlesworth-Smith D *et al*. More care, less pathway: a review of the Liverpool Care Pathway. London: Department of Health, 2013.

Appendix 8

Recommended Summary Plan for Emergency Care and Treatment (ReSPECT)

i Abstract of original publication announcing ReSPECT process and form

Development of the Recommended Summary Plan for Emergency Care and Treatment (ReSPECT)

Claire A Hawkes, Zoe Fritz, Gavin Deas, Sam H Ahmedzai, Alison Richardson, David Pitcher, Juliet Spiller, Gavin D Perkins, ReSPECT working group collaborators

Abstract

Introduction:

Do-not-attempt-cardiopulmonary-resuscitation (DNACPR) practice has been shown to be variable and sub-optimal. This paper describes the development of the Recommended Summary Plan for Emergency Care and Treatment (ReSPECT). ReSPECT is a process which encourages shared understanding of a patient's condition and what outcomes they value and fear, before recording clinical recommendations about cardiopulmonary-resuscitation (CPR) within a broader plan for emergency care and treatment.

Methods:

ReSPECT was developed iteratively, with integral stakeholder engagement, informed by the Knowledge-to-Action cycle. Mixed methods included: synthesis of existing literature; a national online consultation exercise; cognitive interviews with users; a patient-public involvement (PPI) workshop and a usability pilot, to ensure acceptability by both patients and professionals.

Results:

The majority (89%) of consultation respondents supported the concept of emergency care and treatment plans. Key features identified in the evaluation and incorporated into ReSPECT were: The importance of discussions between patient and clinician to inform realistic treatment preferences and clarity in the resulting recommendations recorded by the clinician on the form. The process is compliant with UK mental capacity laws.Documentation should be recognised across all health and care settings. There should be opportunity for timely review based on individual need.

Conclusion:

ReSPECT is designed to facilitate discussions about a person's preferences to inform emergency care and treatment plans (including CPR) for use across all health and care settings. It has been developed iteratively with a range of stakeholders. Further research will be needed to assess the influence of ReSPECT on patient-centred decisions, experience and health outcomes.

ii Current version of ReSPECT form (as of 06.10.22)

ReSPECT **Recommended Summary Plan for Emergency Care and Treatment**

Full name
Date of birth
Address
NHS/CHI/Health and care number

1. This plan belongs to:

Preferred name

Date completed

The ReSPECT process starts with conversations between a person and a healthcare professional. The ReSPECT form is a clinical record of agreed recommendations. It is not a legally binding document.

2. Shared understanding of my health and current condition

Summary of relevant information for this plan including diagnoses and relevant personal circumstances:

Details of other relevant care planning documents and where to find them (e.g. Advance or Anticipatory Care Plan; Advance Decision to Refuse Treatment or Advance Directive; Emergency plan for the carer):

I have a legal welfare proxy in place (e.g. registered welfare attorney, person with parental responsibility) - if yes provide details in Section 8   ☐ **Yes** ☐ **No**

3. What matters to me in decisions about my treatment and care in an emergency

Living as long as possible matters most to me	Quality of life and comfort matters most to me

What I most value:	What I most fear / wish to avoid:

4. Clinical recommendations for emergency care and treatment

Prioritise extending life	Balance extending life with **or** comfort and valued outcomes **or**	Prioritise comfort
clinician signature	clinician signature	clinician signature

Now provide clinical guidance on specific realistic interventions that may or may not be wanted or clinically appropriate (including being taken or admitted to hospital +/- receiving life support) and your reasoning for this guidance:

CPR attempts recommended Adult or child	For modified CPR **Child only, as detailed above**	CPR attempts **NOT** recommended Adult or child
clinician signature	clinician signature	clinician signature

www.respectprocess.org.uk

Version 3.0 © Resuscitation Council UK

5. Capacity for involvement in making this plan

Does the person have capacity to participate in making recommendations on this plan? Document the full capacity assessment in the clinical record.

☐ **Yes**
☐ **No**

→ If no, in what way does this person lack capacity?

If the person lacks capacity a ReSPECT conversation must take place with the family and/or legal welfare proxy.

6. Involvement in making this plan

The clinician(s) signing this plan is/are confirming that (select A,B or C, OR complete section D below):

☐ **A** This person has the mental capacity to participate in making these recommendations. They have been fully involved in this plan.

☐ **B** This person does not have the mental capacity, even with support, to participate in making these recommendations. Their past and present views, where ascertainable, have been taken into account. The plan has been made, where applicable, in consultation with their legal proxy, or where no proxy, with relevant family members/friends.

☐ **C** This person is less than 18 years old (16 in Scotland) and (please select 1 or 2, and also 3 as applicable or explain in section D below):

☐ **1** They have sufficient maturity and understanding to participate in making this plan

☐ **2** They do not have sufficient maturity and understanding to participate in this plan. Their views, when known, have been taken into account.

☐ **3** Those holding parental responsibility have been fully involved in discussing and making this plan.

D If no other option has been selected, valid reasons must be stated here: (Document full explanation in the clinical record.)

7. Clinicians' signatures

Grade/speciality	Clinician name	GMC/NMC/HCPC no.	Signature	Date & time
Senior responsible clinician:				

8. Emergency contacts and those involved in discussing this plan

Name (tick if involved in planning)		Role and relationship	Emergency contact no.	Signature
Primary emergency contact:	☐			optional
	☐			optional
	☐			optional
	☐			optional
	☐			optional

9. Form reviewed (e.g. for change of care setting) and remains relevant

Review date	Grade/speciality	Clinician name	GMC/NMC/HCPC No.	Signature

If this page is on a separate sheet from the first page: **Name:**   **DoB:**   **ID number:**

www.respectprocess.org.uk

 **Recommended Summary Plan for Emergency Care and Treatment**

Discussion guide

People have different views about what care or treatments they would want if they were suddenly ill and could not make choices. ReSPECT conversations allow a person and their health professionals to plan together for such a future emergency. If a person does not have capacity to participate, ReSPECT conversations should include their legal proxy (if they have one), family members or other carers.

 Ensure that all involved in the conversation understand the purpose of ReSPECT.

Start the ReSPECT process with one or more conversations between each person and their health professionals to establish and record in **section 2** a shared understanding of the person's present condition or situation and how these might change....

 Next, discuss, agree and record in **section 3** those things that the person thinks would matter most to them (values and fears) if they suddenly became less well, both in their daily lives and as a possible outcome of future emergency care and treatment.

| Living as long as possible matters most to me | Quality of life and comfort matters most to me |

Using the scale may help you to discuss and agree priorities. Use the discussed / agreed goals of care to guide further planning discussions

 Then discuss, agree and record in **section 4** recommendations about those types of care or realistic treatment that:

- would be wanted (to try to achieve the goals of care),
- would not be wanted,
- that would not work in this person's situation.

As part of this, discuss, agree and record a recommendation about CPR.

www.respectprocess.org.uk

 **R❤SPECT** Recommended Summary Plan for Emergency Care and Treatment

Guidance for people with a ReSPECT form

Now you have a ReSPECT form, what next?

Keep it somewhere easy to find

Make sure your ReSPECT form will be easy to find if you were to become ill and need emergency care. Keep it in a prominent place when you are at home, and take it with you if you are out and about. It will help if your family or carers know where to find your ReSPECT form in case you are unable to access it yourself in an emergency.

Take it to medical appointments

So that your health professionals know your preferences, take the form with you to medical appointments or if you are admitted to hospital. It is your form to keep hold of, though it may be scanned for record keeping or audit.

Review your plan with your health professionals

You can and should review with your health professionals the recommendations on the form if your health condition, circumstances or wishes change. This is to make sure that the plan is kept up to date so that clinicians can make the best possible decisions about your care in an emergency.

Tell your close family, friends and carers about your plan

If your family, friends and carers know about your plan before you need emergency care, they will be able to advise any clinicians treating you and show them your ReSPECT form. Remember to tell family, friends and carers what has changed, if your ReSPECT form is updated.

Frequently asked questions
for patients, carers, and treating clinicians.

Is it legally binding?

No. A person's ReSPECT form contains recommendations to guide immediate decision-making by health or care professionals who respond to them in an emergency. However, they should have valid reasons for not following the recommendations on a ReSPECT form. The ReSPECT form is not an Advance Decision to Refuse Treatment (ADRT).

Is ReSPECT the same as a DNACPR (Do Not Attempt CPR) form?

No. A person's ReSPECT form makes recommendations about emergency treatments that could be helpful and should be considered, as well as those that are not wanted by or would not work for them. It includes a recommendation about CPR, but that may be a recommendation that CPR is attempted, or a recommendation that it is not attempted.

Who needs to sign the form?

The health professional must sign the form to confirm their responsibility in adhering to best practice, following the ReSPECT process and for complying with capacity and human rights legislation. Patients, or their legal proxy and/or family members, can sign the form if they wish but do not have to. Signing the form allows patients or their legal proxy/family members to demonstrate that they have been actively involved in the discussion and recommendations about the person's care and treatment.

How do I get advice or more information?

You can get more information at www.respectprocess.org.uk, or by asking your GP or hospital doctors.

Appendix 9

i. Health and Care Act Bill 2022

Extracts from Health and Care Bill during progress through Parliament:

(a) Baroness Professor Finlay's original proposed amendment and

(b) final accepted Government (Lord Kamal's) amendment

a. Baroness Professor Finlay's original proposed amendment

Lead member

Baroness Finlay of Llandaff
Crossbench, Life peer, Lords

Decision

Not moved
This amendment was not moved – the House was not invited to take a decision on it.

Amendment text
In Clause 16, Page 14, line 23

at end insert—

"3ZA **Further provision in relation to palliative care**

(1) For the purposes of section 16 "specialist palliative care services" must include the provision of—

   (a) support in every setting including private homes, care homes, hospitals, hospices and other community settings, working with local clinical teams,

   (b) hospice and other palliative care beds when required, including admission on an urgent basis,

   (c) specialist palliative care advice, available at all times of day every day,

   (d) support to ensure the right, skilled workforce, equipment and medication is available to deliver this care,

   (e) support by telephone from specialist healthcare professionals,

(f) a point of contact, available for people with palliative and end of life care needs if their usual source of support is not accessible,

(g) appropriate systems to share information about the person's needs with all professionals involved in their care, provided they give consent for this,

(h) support for advance care planning development in all services to ensure patients are able to have open conversations about their needs and concerns,

(i) support for the education and training of the health and social care workforce, and

(j) support to enable staff to participate in relevant research and advance innovations in palliative care.

(2) Palliative care is an approach that—

(a) improves the quality of life of patients (adults and children) and their families who are facing problems associated with life-threatening illness,

(b) prevents and relieves suffering through the early identification, correct assessment and treatment of pain and other problems,

(c) prevents and relieves suffering of any kind, including physical, psychological, social or spiritual, experienced by adults and children living with life-limiting health problems, and

(d) promotes dignity, quality of life and adjustment to progressive illnesses, using best available evidence."

Member's explanatory statement

This amendment is consequential to the amendment at page 13, line 38. It defines palliative care as stated by the World Health Organisation and stipulates the specific services provided by specialist palliative care to support the health and care system to achieve the aims set out in the WHO definition.

Sponsors

Lord Hunt of Kings Heath, Labour, Life peer
Baroness Hodgson of Abinger, Conservative, Life peer
The Lord Bishop of Carlisle, Bishops

b. Final accepted Government (Lord Kamal's) amendment

Lead member

Lord Kamall
Conservative, Life peer, Lords

Decision

Agreed
This amendment was agreed to. Where a member has opposed a Clause standing part of a Bill, 'agreed' indicates that the Clause was removed from the Bill.

Amendment text
In Clause 16, Page 13, line 42

at end insert—

"(ga) such other services or facilities for palliative care as the board considers are appropriate as part of the health service,"

Member's explanatory statement

This amendment would specifically require integrated care boards to commission such services or facilities for palliative care (including specialist palliative care) as they consider appropriate for meeting the reasonable requirements of the people for whom they have responsibility.

ii. Extract from:

Statutory Guidance for Integrated Care Boards (ICBs).
NHS Palliative and End of Life Care, Issued 20 July 2022

(Publication approval reference: PAR1673)

The legal requirement on ICBs

The core responsibility for commissioners is to commission high quality safe services that are tailored to the needs of the individual. The Health and Care Act 2022 states a legal duty on ICBs to commission palliative care services under s3(1) NHS Act 2006 (as amended):

(1) An integrated care board must arrange for the provision of the following to such extent as it considers necessary to meet the reasonable requirements of the people for whom it has responsibility—

(h) such other services or facilities for palliative care as the board considers are appropriate as part of the health service

The duty is intended to ensure that the palliative and end of life care needs of people of all ages, with progressive illness or those nearing the end of their lives, and their loved ones and carers, receive the care and support they need to live and to die well.

All organisations who provide palliative and end of life care should understand and ensure that they comply with their other legal duties and professional obligations. This includes addressing health inequalities for PEoLC, by improving equity of access to underserved populations.